# Go Deliver!

## The Blythswood Story

David Porter

Christian Focus Publications

ISBN 1 85792 000 7

Published by
Christian Focus Publications Ltd
Geanies House, Fearn, Ross-shire,
IV20 1TW, Scotland, Great Britain.

Cover design by Donna Macleod
Cover photograph by Andrew Allan, Alness

Contents

## Foreword

This account of the work of Blythswood has been written with the full co-operation and generous assistance of Jackie and Elma Ross and various others who have been involved with the Society since it began in 1966. On my several visits to Scotland I have been given every help and access to all records and individuals at Blythswood's premises at Lochcarron, Dingwall and Alness. I am particularly grateful for hospitality given by Jackie and Elma and their family, which has made this a very enjoyable project. Practical help, hospitality and much background information has been provided by my publishers, Christian Focus Publications, whose beginnings are recorded in the story that follows.

I have drawn on the Society's records, interviews with key people, and other resources such as the video produced by HCVF Videos about the work of Blythswood. I have also been given help by Presbyterian ministers and by organisations active in Eastern Europe. Where I use the present tense, I am referring to the late summer of 1992.

I have drawn upon my own experiences of travelling extensively in Hungary and Romania since 1989, and have made use of standard reference works. I have used as a basic reference the authoritative study by Janice Broun, *Conscience and Captivity: Religion in Eastern Europe* (Ethics & Public Policy Centre: Washington, 1988), which remains an invaluable guide even though the regimes it describes have fallen. By a pleasant coincidence, Janice Broun lives in Scotland. I have also been helped and moved by Philip Ross's written accounts of his numerous trips on Blythswood convoys: this book owes a great deal to his insights.

My wife Tricia has transcribed many hours of taped interviews and has made many valuable suggestions; this project has been very much a partnership.

Because much of Blythswood's work involves people who are living in countries currently at war, or in which to be a committed Christian is still a cause for harassment, I have changed the names and personal details of one or two individuals in Eastern Europe. There are some invented characteristics, but all the incidents recorded in the book actually happened.

It is perhaps worth emphasising here a point that is made several times in the story that follows; Blythswood works entirely through official channels and internationally recognised agencies, does not contravene the laws of the countries to which it delivers aid, and does not attempt to introduce Bibles or any other Christian literature into any country illegally.

This book could not have been written without the contributions of many individuals and agencies. Any shortcomings, however, are my responsibility and not that of those who have helped me.

# Introduction: Good News from a Far Land

> Out in the little kirkyard our forefolk sleep; birds sing joyously in the wood close by. From the hill, far off, remote, un-domestic, comes the cry of the muir-fowl, the haunting cry of the snipe and the fretful wail of the curlew - owls hoot eerily in the evenings, and bats fare forth on their secret ways; but the predominating note is one of quiet peacefulness. (Isabel Cameron, *The Doctor and his Friends*, 1938)

In the tea rooms in the row of shops that passes for Lochcarron's main street they offer you a choice of Earl Grey, Lapsang or Indian tea bags; a trolley of home-made cakes and a sideboard with brochures advertising local tourist attractions complete the cosy scene. You may have to persuade the cat to vacate the most comfortable chair, and your view of the loch will probably be blocked by passers-by pausing to chat on the narrow pavement outside, but it's an enjoyable spot in which to relax on a holiday morning. The proprietor comes from Manchester. She's a friendly woman who likes to chat with her customers; she'll tell you how much she likes the tranquillity, the slower pace of life, the agreeable local people - everything anyone would want to emigrate to the Scottish highlands for, in fact.

Outside, the hills brood magnificently over the small village and the deep waters of the loch. Rough-carpeted in heather and scrub, they change dramatically several times a day in different lights and different weathers - radiantly crowned in sunshine, draped in shifting shadows in the all-night twilight of high summer, or veiled in elusive dark browns and violets in the soft drizzle that visits the region regularly.

Except for the tartan souvenirs and the unmistakably Highland loch, you could be in the Tatra mountains in Poland, the Slovenian Alps in Yugoslavia, or the foothills of the Fagaras mountains in south-east Romania.

Lochcarron is a small village, 250 miles north of Glasgow on the west coast of Scotland near to the Island of Skye; it is situated in a sheltered spot on the shore of the sea-loch from which it takes its name. Much liked by tourists, Lochcarron appears in many guide-books; just inland, there is good walking to be had among the hills. The great travel writers tended to leave the village off their itinerary. H.V. Morton passed to the south of the loch, Dr Johnson went even further south to sail to Skye from Glenelg; John Hillaby, one of the few modern travellers likely to be read fifty years from now, chose Dr Johnson's route north and missed Lochcarron too.

Unemployment is low and the people are hard-working. Some work for the Forestry Commission and some are crofters. The main industry is fish farming, which employs a large number of local people. In the old days sea fishing was the major industry. Two centuries ago in 1776 Lochcarron was a thriving fishing port when a schoolmaster from nearby Applecross took up a post in the village and later became its Presbyterian pastor. Lachlan Mackenzie was to become Lochcarron's most famous son, known throughout the Highlands, engaged in many church controversies, a central figure in a great Christian revival in Scotland, and the subject of a biographical anthology, *The Happy Man*[1].

Today Lochcarron is in the news again. Not for the reputation of its Presbyterian minister - though a Presbyterian minister from Lochcarron is at the heart of the story told in this book, and was honoured as 1991's Scot of the Year - nor for the glories of its scenery and its tourist attractions, though the village still thrives as a magnet for holidaymakers. Today, Lochcarron is known through-

1. Iain Murray (ed.), *The Happy Man: the Abiding Witness of Lachlan Mackenzie* (Banner of Truth Trust, 1979).

out Scotland and much further afield as the place where an extraordinary organisation has its headquarters, which from tiny beginnings has grown to an operation spanning three continents and beyond.

The organisation began with the unlikely name of The Blythswood Tract Society. This is its story.

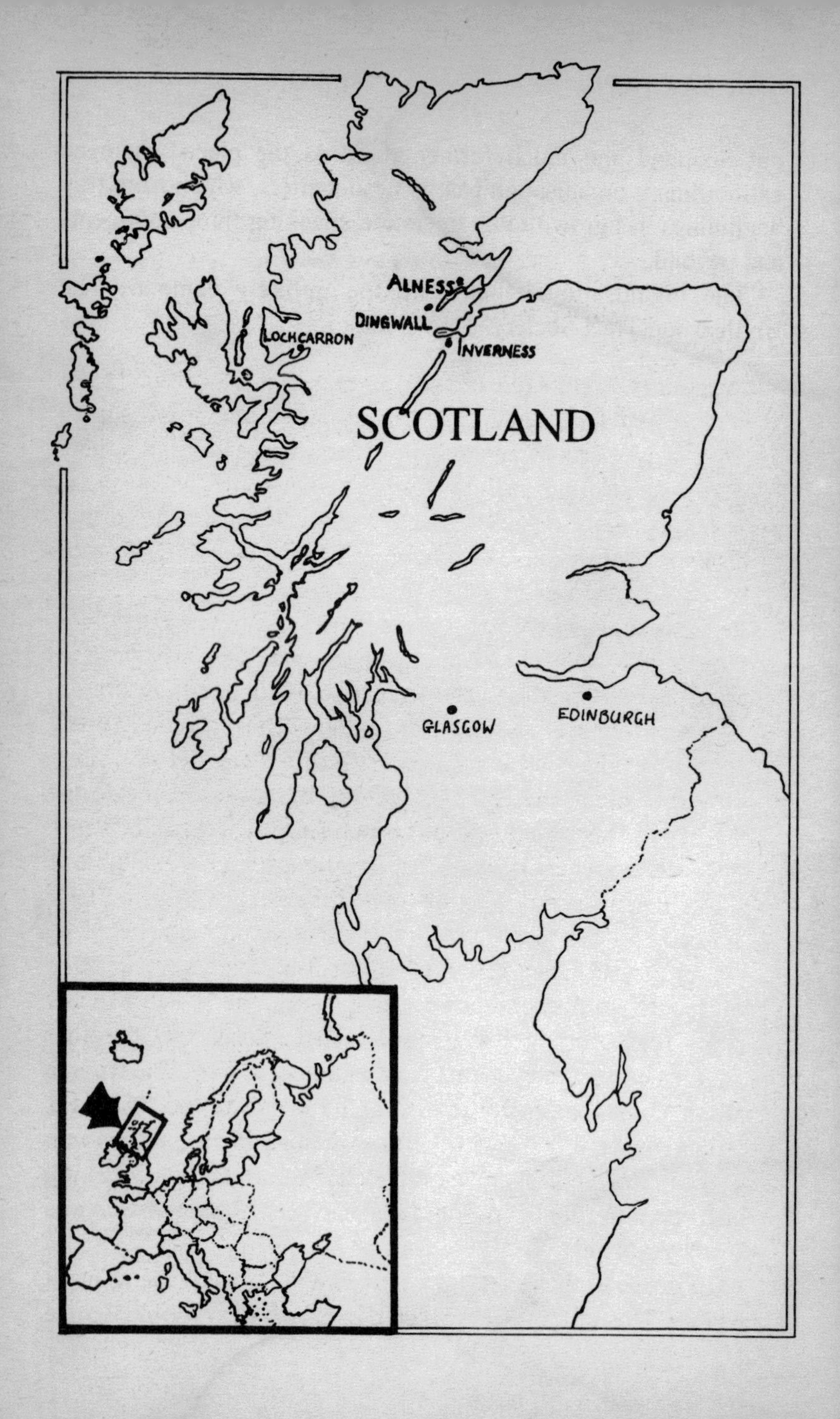
SCOTLAND
ALNESS
DINGWALL
LOCHCARRON
INVERNESS
GLASGOW
EDINBURGH

# 1
# Some Snapshots of Blythswood

Wagons roll ... and five lorry-loads of desperately needed aid hits the road for Romania. The mercy convoy was leaving the little West Coast village of Lochcarron this morning on the 1,000-mile trip across European roads. They are filled, thanks to the generosity of the Highlands and the North-East. ('North Convoy to Romania', *Press and Journal*, 6 March 1991)

When the church was destroyed, the great bell crashed to the floor. The person standing under it had no chance. Nobody knew whether it was a priest trying to salvage some precious image or decoration or just a citizen seeking refuge from the shelling. Nobody knew now whether the dead body was male or female, old or young, beautiful or plain; the half that had protruded from beneath the fallen bell had been removed and buried. The rest of the body would have to remain where it was. There was no machinery available to begin to repair the building, let alone lift the huge cast iron bell. Machinery, in war-torn Croatia, was a scarce commodity.

He or she had died quickly, at any rate. Like many who died that day they had lain unburied for a long time. The stench of what remained of the rotting flesh mingled with the stench of all the other decaying bodies, but even that was beginning to fade. The woman weeping at the road side was used to the stench anyway. She was weeping for her husband who had been gunned down, her sons who had been carried off, her house which had been burned, her church which was now rubble, its priest who had been murdered. She was seventy years old.

The driver of the relief truck prayed with her, but she wept all the more. Tins of food were given her, but how could she prepare food without a stove and utensils, without even a tin-opener? The interpreter showed her how to open the tins with their aluminium keys, and she gasped at the sight of the corned beef inside. As she hugged the cans the tears flowed even more. The lorries began to move on. The woman clutched the cans and watched the vehicles lurching off on the rough dirt road. She spoke no English and could not read the signs on the vehicles: 'International Family Aid: Blythswood'.

At Dingwall, twenty miles from Inverness on the East coast of Scotland, the steel gates of an industrial complex swung open. A convoy of forty-ton lorries moved from the tarmac forecourt into the main road. In the thin sunlight of the early morning a handful of bystanders waved them off. The lorries were packed with clothes, medicine, food, and Christian literature. Their first destination: Ramsgate on the English coast, 600 miles to the south. Then through Belgium, Germany, Austria and Hungary to Romania, where the people were struggling in the face of yet another bitter winter.

Of those in the cabs, most had made the journey before. Some were on college vacation, some unemployed, some using precious holidays taken from demanding jobs; they knew that the journey was uncomfortable, that roads were often dangerous, that the interminable paperwork and the strain of conveying a valuable cargo through countries still scarred by terrible oppression would make itself known in tensions of all kinds. Few if any were there for the opportunity to see foreign countries and taste the excitement of travel. All were there because they had seen a need and caught a vision; the vision of Blythswood.

Like most of his contemporaries, the student at the modern African university campus in Nigeria could read English without difficulty. He unwrapped the package from Scotland eagerly, ripping open the careful packaging in his haste. With a sigh of satisfaction he took out the Bible it contained.

A lot had happened since he had picked up the leaflet left in the college common room by one of the Christian students. It offered a free English Bible to anybody who requested one. He'd written off that night. Bibles were difficult to get hold of. He was an intellectually inquisitive young man, wanting to compare the claims of a variety of religions before settling on one for himself. He was sceptical about the tribal religions his family had lived by for generations, but that didn't mean he was going to sign up for Islam, Christianity or even New Age ideas without thinking about it. He was a serious-minded young man, and wanted the facts.

When he mentioned to a friend that he'd sent off for a Bible his friend smiled. 'Get you a good price for that, if you like,' he offered. 'Always a demand for Bibles. Cut me in on the deal and leave it to me.'

But he wasn't interested in the black-market in Bibles that thrived on campus. He wanted to read it. In fact, he found he had no option but to read it. He was disappointed at first to receive a slim paperback and a few sheets of paper, but found that it was part of the Bible - the Gospel of Mark and the Book of Acts - and a correspondence course. On the title page of the booklet was the same address that had been on the leaflet: Blythswood, Lochcarron, Ross-shire, Scotland. He'd completed the questions - which involved careful reading of the booklet and some thought - sent them to Scotland, and now his Bible had arrived. Tucked inside was a careful assessment of his work on the text and an invitation to send for further books.

> Many of you have requested a further study course. We have available a Christian book for further study - *Right With God* by John Blanchard. If you would like to receive this book, please complete the form below and return it to us in the envelope provided.[1]

He put the Bible carefully into his briefcase along with his

---

1. *Right with God* is published by The Banner of Truth Trust.

textbooks. He'd certainly had to do some work for it, he thought, and smiled wryly. It would take a very committed black marketeer to build up stocks this way.

The husband and wife struggling with a trolley full of groceries emerged from the check out counter and headed for the car park. At the supermarket exit a trolley was strategically placed, bearing the name and green-leaf logo of Blythswood and an invitation to contribute an item of food to Eastern Europe. The couple looked at it, then at each other. As they went by they put a couple of tins of soup in. The trolley was already more than half full.

In the Alness district of Northern Scotland in the flat lands bordering the Cromarty Firth, the old aeroplane hangars are still standing where seaplanes were housed during the war awaiting their missions. The calm, deep waters of the Firth were ideal for training. Today the hangars are used for a variety of commercial and agricultural purposes. Out in the Firth, oil rigs due for repair and maintenance usually stand looming majestically out of the water into the sky; few sea lochs are deep enough to take them, but the Cromarty waters are safe from North Sea gales and the battering of ocean tides. It's a long time since a seaplane taxied across these deep seas.

One hangar, in the middle of fields at the end of a wartime concrete runway now cracked and overgrown, houses a curious collection of objects. A casual walker discovering it and finding it deserted (unlikely) would have a hard job working out what its purpose was. Here, for example, is a very selective inventory for one summer's day in 1992:

> A twenty-foot mountain of black plastic bags, each containing laundered and sorted clothes labelled for men, women, children, summer or winter.
> An assortment of artificial limbs.
> Several dentist's chairs, hospital chairs, and medical equipment trolleys.

Anaesthesia cylinder trolleys.
Boxes of bric-a-brac, sorted into categories.
Several dozen boxes of children's books.
A folding clothes-horse.
Disposable paper sheets.
White plastic sheets in manufacturers' boxes.
Stacks of mattresses.
A box of fancy shirts, new and shrink-wrapped.
Several zimmer frames.
A clothes rack, bearing a quantity of men's suits.
An electric stove.
Several boot-stretchers.
A number of sewing machines of various vintages.
Several hundred new rubber hot water bottles.
A doll's house, and a child's chamber pot.
Dozens of bags of blankets.

Several forty-ton trucks are parked inside the hangar. At one end of the building are several wrecked vehicles, being stripped down for spares. One is a juggernaut that has jack-knifed and been written off; the engine has been removed and is on a bench alongside it, being cleaned and overhauled. One or two farm tractors are parked there too, and a vehicle set up as a mobile exhibition centre bears the invitation 'Come in and browse!'.

The forty-ton vehicles are being loaded with supplies from the hangar, being packed by a handful of volunteers. As the work goes on, visitors arrive with more goods; sometimes a few small second-hand items, sometimes a major delivery of goods fresh from a factory or store. They are welcomed, their goods recorded and stored in their allocated space in the hangar. In due course they will find their way into the large lorries, gradually filling up. The sign on their sides is bold and prominent:

International Family Aid
BLYTHSWOOD
Help us to help others
Lochcarron, Ross-shire, Scotland

There's a relaxed atmosphere in the hangar, but the workers get on with the task. The building is roughly 160 feet by 90 feet in area. There is not much free space.

Donald Macleod, Blythswood's Appeals Co-ordinator, was showing a journalist round the Dingwall depot a few miles away from Alness. They were standing in a room full of sorted piles of goods. He pointed to two small shabby cases standing between cartons of dried food and a Tandy business computer of dubious vintage. 'There's about fifteen thousand pounds' worth of medical equipment in those suitcases,' he said laconically. Nearby was an anaesthesia kit, all gleaming chrome stand and rubber hoses; several sets of scales and balances (including one complicated contraption for weighing babies); and a mountain of mattresses. 'This is our medical store,' explained Donald. 'We keep stuff here that needs extra security.' Through the doorway into a larger storeroom much more varied items could be glimpsed. Numerous boxes of children's toys piled on shelves, including colourful Fisher-Price activity packs and stacks of jigsaws; on the floor, a carton of second-hand books, with titles like *The Big Book of Adventures* and *Five Go to Kirren Island*. Scythes, spades and other farming implements were propped up in odd corners.

The Dingwall depot, being warmer and drier than the Alness hangar, is used for some goods that need better storage conditions than the hangar can provide. The twenty-four two-litre carboys of 'Simple Linctus BP' and the two suitcases of expensive equipment, the infra-red heat lamp and all the other valuable and desirable medical items, are kept under lock and key in the building, which is itself secure behind high wire fences and padlocked gates. Blythswood did not plan such efficient security and could not afford it even if they had done; the security was installed by the company that used the premises before they were donated to Blythswood. It's one of those fortunate 'accidents' that are familiar to all who know the Blythswood story, though nobody who knows them well would use the word 'coincidence'.

The journalist made notes, accepted a strong cup of tea from one of the volunteers who were working in the storeroom, flicked through a book about Ceausescu's Romania lying on the window-sill, and continued to make notes industriously. He inspected the two small offices crammed into the building which appeared to be already bursting at the seams. The reception area, the first room a visitor would see, was thriving in an ordered chaos supervised by a calmly efficient and unflappable receptionist sitting at a desk among a constant coming and going as helpers arrived to deliver goods or sort them. The interview with Donald Macleod was completed in the inner office, a glass-and-plywood partition that created a corner where interviews with the press and quiet conversation were possible, if liable to interruption. A telephone and a fax machine on the desk, Donald pointed out, were both donated by local well-wishers, as was the photocopying machine in the outer office.

This is an organisation that spreads across several continents and is found in the most diverse circumstances. The children in several primary schools know Blythswood; they have been fund-raising for the children of Eastern Europe for months. Viewers of Grampian television know the Society well, for it is often in the news and a feature-length video has been shown during peak viewing time, of the activities of Blythswood. Its President, Jackie Ross, was awarded the Scot of the Year title in February 1991, an honour awarded by listeners to BBC Radio Scotland; Jackie, a quiet and decidedly modest man whose often sober manner conceals a great sense of fun, is quick to tell you that it was a recognition not so much of any qualities he might have but of what has been achieved by the people who have worked, contributed, planned and prayed for many years to bring Blythswood to its present state. He will produce, as his trump card proving that the honour really has nothing to do with him, the fact that his young son, Jason registered a telephone vote on his behalf in the name of their family cat...

It may seem, especially to the outsider discovering for the first time the scope and diversity of the Society's activities both now and over the years, that Blythswood has grown too big and has its fingers in too many pies. But there is a unity and logic to the operation as a whole that is very clear when one spends time with any of those who have been a part of the leadership and share the vision of Blythswood. To understand the roots of the organisation, both organisationally, geographically and spiritually, it is necessary to go back in time to the beginnings of the Blythswood Tract Society. Those readers who have no taste for Scottish Presbyterian history, or who have no interest or commitment to Christianity or to evangelising those who have as yet not heard the gospel are, of course, free to leave the next two chapters unread. But if you skip the next few pages, you will be missing several important stages in the formation of the Society and leaving yourself without a proper perspective on the history and tiny beginnings of this extraordinary society.

# 2
# Early Days

> *Matters arising*: The visitation of model lodging houses was discussed. It was decided that members, when possible, should visit these houses in pairs, after 6.30 on Wednesday evenings. (Minutes of the Blythswood Tract Society, 8 November 1967)

The family in the Albanian home gathered uneasily in the single ground floor room to welcome the visitors from a distant country. The Blythswood vehicles were parked outside, surrounded by a group of inquisitive villagers kept at a distance by police guarding the vehicle. The police were armed with machine guns.

Inside, Jackie Ross and his helpers were appalled at the standard of living that their hosts had to endure. The whole house had the dull, stale smell of rooms impossible to keep entirely clean. The walls were roughly plastered, probably with animal dung and clay, and in several places large damp stains were spreading from the outside so that the plaster blistered and swelled. *It should really be pulled off*, reflected Jackie, *and the job done properly.* It was a passing thought, quickly discarded as he multiplied this one damp and leaking house with the hundreds of thousands in that part of Albania alone. These were the people who, their leader Enver Hoxha had assured them, enjoyed the highest standard of living in Europe, the envy of all other countries on the continent. In those days, when Albania was effectively sealed to all except occasional tourists following government routes and seeing government-prescribed sights, it was an easy deception to maintain.

The furniture was old and cheap. A few embroidered cloths hung on the wall covered the worst patches and added a touch of human creativity to the room. Jackie felt a tug on his sleeve and became aware that he was being invited to inspect the sleeping recess, away from the main room. Against the far wall of the room a sideboard was placed as centrepiece, a plywood and chipboard veneer construction that was old and scratched. Behind sliding glass doors a few odds and ends had been arranged. In pride of place the family had put their most treasured ornament, and it was this that the visitors were being urged to admire. It was an empty plastic shampoo bottle, English or American, probably scavenged from a hotel dustbin where a tourist had thrown it out.

The visitors had brought food and other necessities from the lorry, and they began to distribute them. The absence of a common language prevented much conversation, though the interpreter who was part of the group did what was necessary. But, as had happened many times on such trips, there was a wealth of communication without spoken words; by smiles, gestures, pointing and nodding, a great deal was said.

As Jackie and his colleagues carried cartons of food into the small house for later distribution in the village and offered medical supplies, he might well have reflected that this was not the first time he had visited the poor and brought food and other relief. In fact he had first been involved in such work many years ago; and not in a dusty Albanian village, but in the dirty side streets of a Glasgow slum.

When the young Jackie Ross decided to train for the Free Presbyterian ministry in the 1960s he knew that there was no theological college or academic institution to which he could apply. The method of training was for young men to be attached to local congregations for periods of a year or more, under the guidance of a senior pastor. They were taught in classes four days a week in three ten-week terms, attended the church, and were used as supply preachers almost every weekend - which might involve them travelling as far north as Wick or as far south as London. Formal theological teaching was given by tutors drawn from the denomination, though training for preaching and pastoral work was less systematically done. It was a system similar to that in operation among the Free Presbyterian churches of Ireland (though there is no organisational link between the two Churches), and while it did not have the prestige - in the eyes of some - of the theological academy training provided by the larger denominations, it was an excellent way of learning by observation and by actually doing the job. It was also a method of teaching that was directly descended from the mediaeval universities, where a scholar might travel half of Europe with one or two students in tow.

Jackie began his training with a modified Arts Course set up by the Free Presbyterian Church and Glasgow University. On completion of the course, six students embarked upon their training together in a small building attached to St Jude's Church, which was given the title of 'The Free Presbyterian College': they would study for three years, based in a different town each year.

A number of remarkable teachers influenced Jackie. At Glasgow, he was tutored in theology by Rev. Donald MacLean. Later he studied Greek with Rev. A. F. MacKay of Inverness, and homiletics and Hebrew with Rev. Malcolm MacSween of Oban. The last had a characteristic mannerism of emphasising certain points by exclaiming 'Gentlemen - *NB*!' His students rapidly discovered that there was a method to his idiosyncrasy: if you memorised all the 'NB' points you were guaranteed a good mark in the examinations. Rev. MacSween's emphasis was based on careful analysis of past questions ...

The Free Presbyterians in the 1960s were - and still are - a minority church: the Presbyterian Church of Scotland - 'the Kirk' - and the Roman Catholic Church between them accounted for over ninety percent of church membership in Scotland. The Free Presbyterians accounted for only a small part of the remainder. The climate of national church life was uneven. Revivals in the North East in 1925 and in the Isle of Lewis in the 1950s, and some signs of church growth in for example the Baptist churches, hardly added up to a thriving spiritual environment; many looked nostalgically back to the mighty spiritual movements of earlier generations and the great Scottish Christians of the past such as missionaries David Livingstone and Mary Slessor and athlete Eric Liddell (later to become famous throughout the world as an example of Christian conscience when his story was filmed as *Chariots of Fire*).

Jackie and some of his fellow pastors-in-training were deeply moved by the spiritual plight of their country and resolved to do something about it. They were especially appalled that there were so many people who seemed to have never been confronted with the challenge of the Bible and presented with an invitation to commit their lives to Jesus Christ. Matters came to a head for Jackie when he met a contemporary, Christian Puritz, who challenged him to scrutinise his own thinking.

'Your problem, Jackie,' he pointed out, 'is that you want people to come into the church to hear the Good News. But people won't just come into church like that. Why should they? What you should be doing, if you're a Christian and you want to change things, is to go out among the people and take the Good News out to them. Then you can invite them to church.'

Jackie was stung by the criticism but was unable to forget it. His friend was right. The society in which he and the Free Presbyterian Church were living was as much a mission field as any dark continent or jungle tribal homeland. Many of his contemporaries, he knew, were indeed sitting 'in darkness and the shadow of death'. The year was 1966: Britain, by tradition and appearance a 'Christian country', was very far from one in reality. It was the era of the rock culture, of Ban-the-Bomb, of the permissive society and many more revolutionary and disruptive movements. It was a youth culture in protest, and what made it more disturbing was the fact that often what the young were protesting about were things that deserved to be protested at: a lifeless church, mouthing platitudes that robbed the gospel of its vigour; a society that had grown complacent and was refusing to listen to its own conscience, far less the new voices of protest from those who refused to see personal security and self-satisfaction as the ultimate goals in life. The churches in Britain where the gospel was being preached in its truth and rigour, and consequently with power and conviction, were very few. Small wonder that thousands of young people and older people too, listening unenthusiastically to the speculations of those who argued that God was dead (and some who said we must be Honest to God), decided that there was nothing in any of the churches to tempt them inside.

Which did not mean that the young and the rebellious were heroes and idealists whose beliefs and lifestyle were always praiseworthy. There was much that was truthful and clear-sighted in the culture, but also much that was selfish, much that was arrogant, and much indeed that was evil. This was the period of widespread drug usage, of the beginnings of the heroin and cocaine plagues, of the disintegration of the family and the emergence of a proselytising homosexual liberation lobby. The society of the mid-sixties was in spiritual turmoil, and needed the word of God desperately.

Jackie began to discuss these issues with others in the church, and confronted them with the same challenge that Christian Puritz had confronted him. 'Let's do it,' he urged. 'Let's print a tract and give it out to people on the streets and invite them to come to church.'

Several with whom he talked were opposed to the idea, partly because it was considered unduly assertive for a young minister-in-training, and partly because they disagreed with the basic premise: they felt that it was the duty of the unbeliever to make his way to church where he could hear the gospel. One ordained minister advised Jackie to be quiet and settle down to his studies; it was, he was assured by several church members, the responsibility of the church leadership to undertake such outreach, not the young people. At one stage he was given a book by the Reformed theologian R.B. Kuyper, *The Glorious Body of Christ*, which expounded at some length the issue of fragmentation in the church and the dangers of proliferating organisations founded because the church was reluctant to take the initiative; Kuyper's position was probably rather more ambivalent than the person who gave it to Jackie realised.

Others shared Jackie's vision and his grief for what he saw as the plight and lostness of the people he saw all around him in the streets. When three or four expressed a willingness to join him in the new project, they decided to go ahead. The proposal that he put to the small group of friends was simple. A series of leaflets should be published, tracts which would present the gospel to the non-churchgoing man and woman. These tracts would be distributed by himself and his helpers. With each tract would be given an invitation to respond to the Society, and an offer of a free Bible would be made to any who wanted to have one. The funds for the enterprise would be raised by donations. The aims of the Society would be (to quote the statement that was printed in due course) 'to invite and encourage people, by means of the publication and distribution of scripturally sound Christian literature, to come to hear the gospel of Jesus Christ preached in its purity.'

Among the small group there was great enthusiasm and a decision to launch the project was made. A confirmation of their decision was a substantial gift of money from an individual in the church, which covered almost all the costs of printing the first tract, a simple statement of the Christian challenge with the title *Hear and Your Soul Shall Live*. It contained an invitation to St Jude's Free Presbyterian Church. When it was finished the ten members of what was to become the Blythswood Tract Society, and later simply Blythswood - its officers in 1967 at the end of the Society's first year were Jackie Ross (President), Alasdair Gillies (Vice-President), D. A. Ross (Jackie's brother, and Honorary Treasurer) and Ian Tallach (Honorary Secretary) - took to the streets and handed them out to passers-by.

For Jackie and his friends it was a vision made reality, though some in the St Jude's congregation and other churches took longer to convince. The first tract *Hear and Your Soul Shall Live* was quickly followed by *God and Man*. News of the project spread, and requests for tracts began to arrive, together with letters from people who had read the tracts and wanted to discuss the contents further. In addition, a new invitation had been added to the tracts: the offer of a free Bible. It was clear that both space and voluntary help would be needed, so the work was established in an inexpensive office, an upstairs room in Glasgow's West Campbell Street near Blythswood Square, and took its name accordingly: the Blythswood Tract Society was in business.

The room was a small one, at the head of a narrow flight of stairs which were awkward to negotiate when parcels had to be carried from the printers or down to the post office. Its single window looked out across a slate roof down to the back yard of the building, and in the early evening prostitutes could be seen looking for customers: the alleys and yards of the district were their territory. Jackie and his friends spent many hours in that room opening parcels of tracts that had come from the printers, sorting out orders and repacking them, answering letters, and dealing with callers; the National Bible Society had premises in the same block, and often their customers would go on up the stairs to purchase tracts or simply to find out what was happening.

For the word was getting around, that the independent-minded students at the Presbyterian church had begun a most interesting and worthwhile ministry. Nor was the church as cautious as it had been; as the work got under way the benefits could be seen both in the outreach to unchurched people and in the lives of those doing the work itself. Others soon joined in who had initially had reservations. One who had had no reservations at all, but had been unable to attend the first meeting, was Ian Tallach, cousin of John Tallach who was already an active worker in the Society. Ian was one of the first members and became Secretary in 1967. John, who had linguistic abilities, was later to play an important part when the Society began to form links with Christian work in Italy.

At the end of its first year, the Society published its first magazine. An 8-page leaflet intended for friends and supporters, bearing the title The *Blythswood Tract Society Magazine*, it had much to report that was encouraging. A wide range of contacts had been made, many of which had resulted in real interest.

Jackie Ross, after his first year as a student in the Glasgow church, was required to spend the next academic year at a Free Presbyterian church in Inverness, studying 'divinity' with Rev. A.F. MacKay in the manse. He continued to work for the Society, travelling back to Glasgow whenever possible. The Society continued to grow: some who had received tracts had visited church; there had been a good response to the offer of free Bibles, some of it coming from Africa; money had been donated, much of it anonymously, and the Trinitarian Bible Society had donated tracts which had been distributed along with the Society's. All sorts of new ideas were being considered to expand the work; a scheme to print large Bible posters was one, another was that lodging houses should be visited in order to distribute literature and evangelise the residents. Open air meetings in Glasgow had begun, too, with the blessing of the Southern Presbytery; often the service coincided with the closing time of the local cinema, which provided a ready-made passing audience. The quantities of tracts being printed were large. In March 1968 a new tract was produced entitled *Do you pray?*, of which 40,000 copies were printed; another, *Hear instruction and be wise* was produced in quantities of 10,000 copies. Another, focusing on particular doctrines and Bible verses, was the product of Society members living in Edinburgh; again, the print run was 40,000. Letters were received from as far afield as Esher in Surrey, Worthing on the South Coast of England, and Gisborne in New Zealand.

Those who were involved in the early days of the Society

remember it as hard but enjoyable work. 'It was a very happy sort of thing,' Jackie recalls. 'Though we used to work ridiculous hours.' In the middle of it all, they became qualified Presbyterian ministers, fitting in New Testament Greek and homiletic studies in between the latest proofs from the printers and a full programme of tract distribution and visiting churches to explain the purpose and the needs of the venture. There was also time for a social life; Jackie became particularly friendly with a red-headed nurse, Elma, whose family were friends of his family. As their friendship deepened, Jackie found many excuses to call at her parents' home.

Anyone who came to know Blythswood a quarter of a century later might be forgiven for looking at the early publications of the Society and thinking that its role in the modern world, with its programme of international aid, represents a complete break from the emphases of the past. But the seeds were present even in those first years in Glasgow.

One significant expansion of the work was the decision to visit 'model lodging houses' in the town. This glamorous title dressed up what were in reality doss-houses. The group decided to take Christian literature to these places and talk to the men who lodged there about Christianity. But it was impossible to separate the urge to proclaim Jesus Christ, which had first prompted them to go to the houses, from the awareness of the poverty in which the men lived. They went to tell the residents that God confronts all people, rich or poor, young or old, with the invitation to make peace with him through the death of his son, Jesus Christ, on the cross for humanity. But none of the Blythswood volunteers who took that gospel into those places could escape being challenged in their turn; a gospel that left its followers unmoved by human misery and deprivation - the evidence of the fall of humanity, to heal which the gospel was given - was hardly a gospel worth proclaiming at all.

The Gorbals and other great slums that had made Glasgow notorious for poverty had long since been swept away by the time that the Blythswood Tract Society was founded. But there was still severe poverty in post-war Glasgow. Jackie and his friends were appalled at the situation of the men they visited. Meetings with them were held in a communal sitting room, whose furniture was rough tables and chairs and a communal cooker. Many of the men accepted the tracts, some probably out of boredom, and there were many conversations that often went on much longer than either party had intended. Reporting the visits in the magazine, Jackie commented on the need such visits revealed, and asked his readers to consider how they could help in some way. It was a beginning; it was to set a direction, albeit in a small way, that was to shape Blythswood's progress for the next three decades. Blythswood members were not just distributors of Christian leaflets. They visited the housebound and the sick; they purchased food and took it those who were hungry and in need; they went to the arches and shadowy corners where the alcoholics and tramps gathered. They saw it as an integral part of their mission. It was, the Blythswood Tract Society believed, nothing out of the ordinary to be doing such things. If you were a Christian, this is what you did. The gospel did not call anybody to a faith that tried to force-feed people's souls while allowing their bodies to suffer and starve.

# 3
# Lochcarron

> Another factor which must induce us to give to the cause of Christ, is love to our fellow-men. Love to Christ leads to love for our neighbour. 'But to do good and [to contribute help] forget not; for with such sacrifices God is well-pleased', Hebrews 13:16. We are not to be forgetful of the needs - especially the spiritual and eternal needs - of our fellow-men. (*The Blythswood Tract Society Magazine*, June 1973)

In 1970 Jackie was ordained as a minister in the Free Presbyterian Church. During his years of training, he had preached at a number of churches. He and his fellow students had become quite well known in various parts of Scotland as rising young men in the ministry. As Jackie came to the end of his studies, invitations began to arrive for him to consider posts at a number of churches.

One invitation was to Shieldaig, a village on the banks of Loch Torridon on the West coast of Scotland, a loch whose waters looked out beyond the northern tip of the Isle of Skye towards the Outer Hebrides. Another came from the village of Lochcarron some fifteen miles south of Shieldaig, across Loch Carron from Kyle of Lochalsh, the main ferry for Skye. Jackie had preached at Lochcarron several times during his student years. It had struck him then as a remote and isolated place, and he had decided that it was the last place in the world that he wanted to live. But now things were different. The attractions of the quiet spot on the loch, the small and friendly community (its population even today is only 790, with a primary school roll of 80) and the chance to escape from the bustle of the big town were all very appealing. It was also, he told himself optimistically, not all that far from Glasgow; Shieldaig, though only

15 miles further north, lay the other side of a mountainous peninsula.

In fact the journey from Lochcarron to Glasgow took three-and-a-half hours; twice a week Jackie would have to leave at six in the morning to get to the Blythswood office by ten. But he was young and enjoyed driving, and the route did after all pass through some of the loveliest landscapes in the British Isles. A continued involvement with the Society was acceptable to the Lochcarron church leaders, too. For the Society it was virtually essential. Nobody is ever indispensable, but Jackie's rare combination of gentleness and business acumen had been a major factor in the development of the work and would have been much missed. He had a title in the organisation which looked very fine on letters and publications: 'John Walter Ross, President'. However, he was fond of pointing out that it was a very small organisation to be president of, and he had been given the title only because people expected an organisation to have a head, and somebody had to do the job.

So he accepted the call to Lochcarron, and became its Free Presbyterian minister in late summer 1970. He did not take up residence in the Manse on his own, for in August of that year he and Elma had been married.

The Rosses enjoyed their new environment. The people of Lochcarron were welcoming and friendly to the family, though reserved about spiritual matters. In later years, when the book van and subsequently the bookshop were opened they were interested, tolerating their appearance in the small village with patient good humour. From the beginning, Jackie and Elma loved the calm waters of the loch and the ever-changing mountains, a dramatic reminder as they went about their daily tasks of the majesty of creation and the providence of God. They made friends among local clergy, too, and other visitors came from farther afield.

Not long after they arrived in Lochcarron, a man lingered at the church door, waiting to speak to the minister. He was a few years older than Jackie, and his manner was forthright. He introduced himself as John Gudgeon, then without further preamble enquired: 'Do you believe in "duty faith"?'

Jackie liked straightforward people and those who, like this direct stranger, came quickly to the point. He pondered the question briefly while John waited for his answer. A Strict Baptist from Harpenden in England who owned a holiday home in Lochcarron, he was curious about the new minister, and wanted to discover his theological position. The 'purity of the faith' was a major concern for him, and he was testing Jackie to find out how he stood in an old controversy.

'Duty faith' was an issue that separated Baptists and Strict Baptists. The latter argued that if some men and women were predestined to damnation and were thereby incapable of faith in Christ - as an interpretation of the Calvinist doctrine of predestination affirmed - then one could hardly urge them to become Christians by telling them that it was their duty to do what they could never do. Like many in his church tradition Jackie considered the issue to be over-philosophical and missing the point of Scripture.

'Yes,' he replied, 'I do. The Bible commands all men everywhere to repent and believe.'

The answer revealed some theological difference of opinion between the two men, and it was an unlikely beginning to what was to become a good friendship. The Reformed churches in Britain have had their share of theological controversy, and feelings can run deep. But both men respected each other's integrity and commitment to Scripture, and continued the conversation over many subsequent meetings. The theological difference between them proved to be less than had first appeared. John was a builder who owned a holiday home in Lochcarron; he had a passion for evangelising Eastern Europe, and was involved in several projects working in that area. An enthusiastic hill walker, he came to Scotland regularly and was a frequent visitor at the Manse. He and his wife became close friends of Jackie, Elma and their family, and, as the story in the pages that follow demonstrates, he was a crucial advisor and guide in the later development of Blythswood's work in Eastern Europe.

The work of Blythswood was to continue from Glasgow for another seven years. New avenues of literature distribution had opened up; for example, as an early outreach to the scattered communities of the Scottish highlands and islands, a 'book van' had been equipped to sell Christian publications. In the summer of 1970 Murdo Maclean, who lived in Glasgow and worked as a journeyman printer, offered his services as full-time representative on the van. It was a step of considerable faith; the Society hoped that his salary, as well as the costs of the upkeep of the vehicle and its driver, would come from the income from literature sales. Unfortunately, the hope was frustrated by the vehicle itself, which was thirteen years old and losing its struggle with the steep hills and rough roads of the Highlands. The winter of 1970 proved too much for it, and in March it was announced that the decision had been made to take the vehicle off the road. The Society's regret was obvious in the brief announcement, and many friends of the work wrote to say how much they hoped that it would be restarted soon. So it was with gratitude and pleasure that the Society recorded in the June magazine that a replacement vehicle had been donated.

The wider ministry of the Blythswood Tract Society continued to grow. In the December magazine correspondence was printed from Blythswood supporters all over Scotland and much farther afield: England, Ireland, France, California, Lagos and many more places. Now that Jackie was based in Lochcarron and only in the office twice a week, there was a need for a full-time secretary who could deal with the mail and the ongoing work of the Society. Jackie was not the only worker whose involvement with the Glasgow office had had to be cut back. Others had moved away or been forced to reallocate their time. The Society began to look in earnest for assistance; Jackie approached several likely people but in every case the person involved was not able to help.

One day a friend asked Jackie, 'Have you spoken to Miss Linden?'

Jackie knew Miss Linden as somebody who attended St Jude's Church, but he had no idea what her background was. When he made enquiries he found that she was a skilled secretary who would be ideal in many ways for the work at the Society's office. Discussing the idea with somebody who knew her, however, he was deflated to be told, 'You're wasting your time. She's in a very good job at McLellan's Rubber Products in Glasgow- she's been with them years.'

It was decided at least to ask Miss Linden, who said that she felt she was not competent to do the work. However, she promised to pray about the offer. Shortly afterwards Jackie was delighted to receive her acceptance. She made a single condition: 'I won't accept any salary from the Society.' She was eligible for early retirement, and chose to take the option so that she could work for the Lord while her needs were met by her pension. Her employers at McLellan's contributed a typewriter and duplicator to help her with the Society's work, a testimonial to the high opinion they had of her long years of service for the firm.

Margaret Linden was efficient and dedicated to the work. She kept a firm control on expenditure, and it is probably from those days that the pattern was set that if funds were not available for a project, the project was held back. Even today, when there is a lull in funds, packages of literature and Bibles are put on one side waiting for the money to post them. She discouraged placing orders with the printers until there was money in the bank to pay for them. She called her new colleagues 'incurable optimists', but her great organisational skills and business common sense did not prevent her from sharing in the Blythswood vision in countless ways. She attended the Free Presbyterian Church, and her wide reading in Reformed literature enabled her to give advice to many who called at the office; she would often be asked why the Society distributed only the Authorised Version of the Bible, and gave sensitive and careful explanations.

Her industry was tireless. She would often stay late to pack a Bible that somebody had asked for, and sometimes she made several trips to the Post Office in one day to ensure that the literature was sent out as soon as possible.

By 1973 there were several book vans on the road: one had been taken to Yorkshire by Walter Gash, a friend of the Society; another operated in the Fort William area, and a third was an ex-County-Library book van parked in the British Legion car park, Inverness. The Society began appealing for further vehicles, encouraged by a number of people who had offered to operate them. Blythswood Christian bookshops were being opened, too; by the end of the year there were three, in Lewis, Skye and Inverness.

The Society's tracts were being read all over the world. In Glasgow itself one Blythswood helper distributed them from a market barrow, but letters poured in too from many countries telling of a hunger for Christian literature and requesting further supplies. At the end of the year, the Society held its first Annual General Meeting. Jackie presented his President's Report for 1973, and reflected upon the major changes that had come over the Society in recent years:

> The Blythswood Tract Society first met in Glasgow, towards the end of 1966. The then members were well acquaint with each other and each was a worker for the Society: every encouragement a mutual joy, every set-back a shared disappointment. While we lived and worked in Glasgow, it was easy for us to be in contact and to discuss Society matters. More recently we have gone our various ways and the original members are now as far apart as the Outer Hebrides, Aberdeen and London, with still further dispersal when our Treasurer goes, God willing, to Rhodesia in mid-February. For this and other reasons some here tonight have not been able to attend meetings for some time, and may feel out of touch with not only our activities but with fellow members. And so the need for an Annual General Meeting seemed apparent, that you might know what is being done and because those who work for the Society require encouragement and direction.

The figures that Jackie presented were encouraging. In 1973 one third of a million tracts had been distributed from the office, the bookshops and the vans. They had gone to Africa, India, Australia, New Zealand, America, Canada, Italy, Iceland and throughout the British Isles. Over 3,300 free Bibles had been distributed, each including a reading scheme. The Bible was one printed for the Society by the Trinitarian Bible Society. Four thousand had been printed, and less then 1,000 remained. In the bookshops, 8,000 customers had been dealt with and 16,000 items sold. Not surprisingly, Jackie found space in his Report for a warm tribute to Margaret Linden: 'How difficult it would be for us to carry on without Miss Linden's help! We would most heartily thank her for her gratuitous work.'

The President's annual report became a regular event, though it has to be remembered that Jackie Ross had only taken on the title to make the Society's note paper look business-like and official; the tone of the reports was never that of an expanding company with an enviable success record, but was always one of profound gratitude to God and a sense of wonder that so much had been accomplished with such slender - in human terms - resources. The 1974 report announced that during the year half a million tracts had been distributed, and that many more distributors had been recruited; many more Bibles had been sent out than during the previous year; and a long-cherished dream of the Society, the setting up of a Bible correspondence course, had become a reality through the voluntary work of a team of markers. The course was now offered to anybody who requested a Bible from the Society. There was steady progress reported, too, from the bookshops and book vans, and the budget for printing tracts and other materials now ran to several thousand pounds.

In 1975 a great increase in Bible distribution was reported, and it was predicted that this would be a particular area of expansion. It was not the only one. In particular, one of the book vans, a caravan, had been attracting steady interest from holidaymakers for several years, who found it a useful place to shelter during occasional showers and frequently stayed on to read and buy; there was also interest from students on vacation. Such was the interest, in fact, that a search had already begun for a mobile office unit which could be used as office, store and shop, thus freeing the caravan for a more mobile ministry once again. The van's location was Lochcarron. Jackie Ross commented wryly, 'On odd occasions, it rains in Lochcarron during the holiday season!'

During 1975, Jackie visited the United States and Canada. As a result of discussions with a number of people over there, the Society was able to report a substantial contribution to the stock of a new Christian bookshop in Vancouver (run by a Scot, Donald Robertson, and his wife), and the appointment of Mr and Mrs Jan Vanderwal as book agents in Toronto. In Kalamazoo in the United States, there were discussions about the setting up of a new Christian bookshop there. At home, there were enquiries from Holland, from Christians who urged the Society to consider beginning a branch of its work there.

To those looking back with hindsight from the far future of the early 1990s, the new directions that were opening up would seem highly significant. In those very early days, most of the pieces of the jigsaw were already in place for what was to become the Society's most publicised and dramatic work, though nobody involved then or now would dream of suggesting that one was more important than the other. Certainly there was no time to stand still and contemplate the future. The work was increasing apace. By 1976, the hoped-for permanent structure at Lochcarron had been found, and the new bookshop opened on 19 March, ahead of schedule; the contacts with Holland, Canada and America were flourishing; and the quantities of Christian literature and Bible being distributed steadily increased. The headquarters of the Society were still in Glasgow, though it was pointed out that the Lochcarron base was contributing substantially to the income of the Society, and Jackie Ross risked a rebuke from one of his most loyal assistants by making the following acknowledgement:

> In spite of requests not to mention her name, we cannot ignore the burden of work borne by Miss Linden in the Glasgow office and bookroom. We take her service so much for granted, and yet the Society's concern is her concern and our rejoicing hers.

In September 1977, a few months after publishing that tribute, the sad news had to be given to the members of the Society that Miss Linden had died peacefully and unexpectedly. The warm tribute to her published in the Blythswood magazine filled a page and a half, and a characteristic portrait of her was placed on its cover.

Major decisions now had to be taken. Should another administrator be sought to take the place of Margaret Linden? Quite apart from natural doubts about whether it would be easy to find somebody who could match the industry, efficiency and spiritual qualities of Miss Linden, other issues had to be faced. Was it right to continue to maintain an office in Glasgow, when costs of property, let alone Jackie's travelling costs and time lost in the twice-weekly journey, were now so considerable? A new administrator might not be able to make the same generous gesture that Miss Linden had, of working without pay. What would the effect of a further full-time salary be on the carefully-balanced finances of the Society, already striving to keep its overheads as low as possible so that the bulk of its resources could be devoted to Christian work?

The answer was obvious. Lochcarron was the Ross's home. The bookshop there had recently moved into a building that was already designed to provide office space as well as a shop area. Its prominence in the work justified a strategic relocation of the headquarters.

So it was announced that the Glasgow office would be closed, at least for the time being, and that mail would be redirected to Lochcarron. The Glasgow workload would be shared between the three staff at Lochcarron: Mrs Mary MacLeod was a formidably efficient office secretary who in many ways resembled Margaret Linden; she had great loyalty to the Society, often working late to make sure that the literature would go out as soon as possible, and like Miss Linden she was gifted in talking with the many people who called at the shop often pretending to browse but in reality looking for spiritual counsel. She worked for Jackie before the bookshop was built, dealing with correspondence, filing and office administration in Jackie's crowded study in a manse that was already filling up with the Rosses' growing family.

When the bookshop was built she was joined by Mrs Cathie Mackenzie, and when the Society's accounts were moved to Lochcarron they were joined by Mrs Florence MacLean whose specific responsibility would be the book agent account system that had previously been managed by Miss Linden. At that time it was realised that the new building would be inadequate, and the only possibility was to clear a huge mound of earth that lay behind it and erect a second building next to the first. Financially, it made sense, as purchase was much cheaper than rent and the new premises could be expected to pay for themselves in a very short time. Jackie and a team of helpers rolled up their sleeves and picked up their shovels. The startled Free Presbyterians of Lochcarron became accustomed to the sight of their minister engaged in labour which to some seemed extremely unecclesiastical!

The move to Lochcarron had advantages that only became apparent when the work was under way there, though they had been a factor in deciding to make the move. For example, in Glasgow the Society had been a small organisation in a town that had many large businesses, some international, multi-million dollar enterprises. In Lochcarron, the Society was a major organisation. Whereas in Glasgow the regular trips to the Post Office involved carrying heavy loads of letters and parcels, queuing at the counter and laboriously dealing with each item - buying stamps, licking each one and sticking it on the parcel or envelope - in Lochcarron it was possible to have a mail contract and arrange for a Post van to call at the office. And it was easier to find voluntary help in Lochcarron than in Glasgow, which at that time had quite high employment so that few people had spare time to give to the work. In Lochcarron there were retired people and some who would donate a Saturday morning or a weeknight evening to the work. In Lochcarron, too, there was a much stronger sense of a Christian community than in the more impersonal environment of Glasgow; the various churches had good relationships with each other and were willing to collaborate in helping enterprises like the Society. In the summer, as the relationship between the Society and its Dutch friends grew, visitors from Holland often arrived to help, too. In the small holiday resort it was always possible to find a pleasant camping site - something that would have been impossible in Blythswood Square, Glasgow.

There was one more reason why Lochcarron was, in the providence of God, a far-sighted choice for the Society's headquarters. There would come a time when vehicles would come and go from the Society, to outlying islands, to mainland villages, and further afield, further than anybody yet imagined. In Lochcarron there were garage premises and somewhat better parking facilities. In Glasgow, it would have proved a major problem.

We must move swiftly through the story of the next decade, for a book that would describe the ramifications of the work, the encouragements and trials and a fraction of the human lives touched by the Society's work would be a different book and a much larger one. But two things stand out, looking back through the pile of Blythswood magazines that are the only public record of a work that was growing and diversifying throughout that period.

Firstly, Jackie Ross would be the first to say that the story of those years is not the Jackie Ross story, nor even the story of a team of dedicated and sacrificial workers, some based in Lochcarron and others spread over Scotland and farther afield. The Presidential reports for those years consistently display a humility and thankfulness that refuses to give the credit to any of the remarkable human beings involved, but solely to the providence and goodness of God.

Somebody to whom the Society owed a great deal but who generally remained in the background was the Secretary, Ian Tallach. Ian had become a licensed preacher in 1972 and had settled in Perth. He was a quiet, learned man who loved books and reading. His main love was history, and when he was a student he had found it very easy to be distracted from his Greek studies by the lure of a desirable historical treatise; he was often to be seen in the Mitchell Library in Glasgow poring over weighty historical tomes. He was a night person, often reading on into the small hours and rising late in the morning. 'He was somebody who was always available, even if you called late, and always keen to talk about what he had been reading,' recalls Jackie.

Ian often arrived at Lochcarron in the early afternoon to work through Blythswood Society business with Jackie, leaving sometimes at five in the morning. They were stimulating and challenging visits. Once Ian had decided a task should be undertaken he set about it with dogged determination, but he did so with considerable vision; he saw potential for the Society to expand in numerous ways; when he was sometimes not able to enthuse others he was often discouraged.

One project in which Jackie was involved found an immediate response in Ian. At the time of the move to Lochcarron, Jackie and some of his friends were exploring the possibility of publishing books as well as tracts. 'Christian Focus Publications' was the result, a publishing venture launched in much the same way as the Blythswood Tract Society had been - by the vision and enthusiasm of a small group. The address of Christian Focus (118 Academy Street, Inverness) was that of the Inverness Blythswood bookshop. The first books published were *A Basket of Fragments* and *The Beauties of Boston*. Both were anthologies drawn from Reformed literature; the former was a collection of the sermons of Robert Murray McCheyne, a nineteenth-century Church of Scotland preacher, hymnwriter and missionary strategist; the latter was not (as one might think) an American travel guidebook but a selection from the works of Thomas Boston, an eighteenth-century Scots Presbyterian writer of whom a classic biography is still widely read[1]. The books were well received, but even Jackie was forced to admit that there was a limit to what could be done with very limited capital and time. They discussed the situation with the Mackenzie family, who among many other business interests owned a printing firm, and it was decided that the Mackenzies should take over the fledgling publishing house with William Mackenzie as Managing Director. Today Christian Focus is a Christian publishing house with a large and varied list and a reputation extending beyond Scotland. It is located in Geanies House at Fearn near Tain, from where Roderick and William Mackenzie conduct their business and their brother Hugh looks after the family farms; another brother, Kenneth, played a major part in the development of Christian Focus. Roderick has played a significant role in the development of Blythswood, having been its Treasurer for many years.

The second thing that stands out in a story that has its own intrinsic interest is that in ways which must at the time have seemed often unconnected, the groundwork was being laid for future work in Eastern Europe. The work of sending free Bibles, literature and correspondence courses to Africa continued; contacts with America and Canada were made and strengthened; but in parts of Europe where the Society had not had previous contact, relationships were established and resources quietly provided which could only have made sense to One who knew the future and what future needs would be.

---

1. George H Morrison, *Memoirs of Thomas Boston* (1899) Available today in an edition published by Banner of Truth. The Banner of Truth also publish Andrew Bonar, *Memoirs and Remains of Robert Murray McCheyne* (1862).

# 4
# The First Links with Foreign Countries

> Friction between Croats and Serbs was a constant hindrance to the peaceful development of Yugoslavia, and has even resulted in internecine warfare within that country during the present war. (J. F. Horrabin, *An Atlas of Post-War Problems*, 1943)

Ljubuski was blacked out; the houses were shuttered and dark. In the small town at the foot of a Hercegovinan valley a few miles from Mostar - on the battle front of the 1992 Serbian offensive in what was once Yugoslavia - the streets were gloomy alleys of blackness, relieved only by moonlight and the lights of occasional coffee bars, inexplicably bright and cheerful in a town at war.

A Blythswood team of volunteer lorry drivers and helpers was sitting drinking coffee with a Croatian friend who was acting as their translator. They were being told tales of the war; of how the soldiers came back from the front bearing trophies of severed ears and fingers taken from enemy corpses. By now the team, after several trips to the region, had heard stories of atrocities on both sides; of shelled hospitals, terrorist atrocities that seemed to be part of no strategic operation, infants and women exposed to horrifying risks. The Serbs blamed the Croats, the Croats the Serbs. As the struggle wore painfully on, the flood of refugees fleeing demolished homes and towns continued, seeking shelter in refugee camps and even caves in the mountains. Their Croat friend was talking of revenge, of reprisals against a deliberate attempt to demolish a hospital. The team had heard almost identical talk from Serbs outraged at alleged Croat atrocities: 'Funnily enough,' one reported on his return, 'the Croats were speaking about the Serbs in exactly the same way that the Serbs were speaking about the Croats last December when we went through Serbia.'

In the restaurant the atmosphere was almost like a carnival; soldiers returning from the fighting around Mostar were drinking and laughing, and the lights were burning bright. 'When do you think the war will end?' asked one of the Scottish visitors. The Croat translator smiled. 'Not when the United Nations tell us it must stop,' he said. 'They're just getting in the way. What's going on here must find it's own end. The fighting will stop then, when all the bloodletting is completed. If you stop the war prematurely, the aggressors will not just go home ... But I hope there will be peace one day.' He picked up his glass and saluted the team with a wry smile. One of them raised his cup hesitantly in return. 'Cheers.'

'*Don't do that*!'

There was fear in the Croat's voice as he looked anxiously round the restaurant. 'That's a Serbian thing to do. We just bang our glass on the table.'

In the street outside a sudden squeal of brakes was a welcome distraction. A car had stopped. The couple who got out were dramatically dressed in black; the young man in black T-shirt and khaki jeans, the girl in a black top and trousers. Both were wearing heavy army boots and had large revolvers pushed casually into their belts. They strode into the coffee bar with only a brief glance at the people there. Then they went through into a small room at the back. The door closed behind them; there was an audible gasp of relief. People began to talk again but in low voices.

'*Hos*,' explained the Blythswood's Croatian translator, nodding towards the closed door. The group of Britishers around him understood immediately. Hos was an extreme Croat paramilitary group, generally considered to be a law unto itself; capable of going into villages and assassinating anybody they chose. It was safer to say nothing when Hos members were around; a careless remark - such as thoughtlessly using the word 'Yugoslavia' - might mean you would be hustled into the back yard and summarily shot.

The couple emerged after half an hour and drove off. Those who had not quietly slipped away in the meantime began to laugh and joke again. The Croat translator frowned at the team. 'If they had seen you raise your cup,' he said, 'they would probably have taken you out and shot you.'

The Blythswood convoy was delivering aid under the auspices of the International Red Cross. Their destination was a town on the other side of the Bosnian border - a border that like many others had been redrawn several times during the fighting. It happened that this time they were delivering humanitarian aid to Croats; other Blythswood convoys had taken aid to Serbs. In the confused and tangled politics of the Balkans, Blythswood is neutral, taking help to those in need. Neutrality in this war is no guarantee of safety; Red Cross convoys have been fired upon and even aid arriving by air has been shelled. But so far Blythswood has been fortunate, both because of its policy of not exposing its volunteers to unnecessary risks and because, they would certainly say, of the providence of God.

It might all seem an enormous departure from the days when Blythswood's role was printing, packing and distributing tracts and Bibles. But it is all part of the same story. Nor did a commitment to the Balkans begin only with the outbreak of hostilities in the early 1990s. Blythswood's involvement with Yugoslavia goes back many years; in fact, to 1977 when the first contacts were made.

In that year a visitor to Yugoslavia gave a Bible to somebody he met. Inside, he placed a Blythswood tract. In due course a letter arrived at Lochcarron requesting a Bible.

From that small beginning, many letters followed and many Bibles were sent. At that time it was costly to be a believer in Yugoslavia, and sometimes even to show an interest was dangerous. The country was an oddity among Communist states. Its leader Marshall Tito had acknowledged the importance of religion in the mixed ethnic population of the region, and had never attempted to eradicate it. Yugoslavia, for example, became in 1970 the first Communist country to officially recognise the Vatican. It had a thriving tourist trade which brought thousands of Western visitors to its six republics each year. There was a measure of national prosperity, and for many foreigners Yugoslavia was the acceptable face of Marxist society, though its political relationship with the West was always somewhat ambiguous.

But the exterior image of an enlightened, tolerant society masked deep troubles that simmered very near the surface. In the 1970s the dialogue between Marxism and religion that had been encouraged in the 1960s began to disintegrate, particularly in the wake of the 'Croat Spring' of 1970-71 in which a surge of Croatian nationalism was met by a wholesale purge by Tito. The consequence for the churches was that the Roman Catholic Church was labelled as a Croat nationalist church, with predictable political effect.

At that time a Christian revival was taking place in Yugoslavia, especially among the young, but the regime responded by placing restrictions on religious freedom and closing a number of youth organisations. The atmosphere of apparent toleration cooled, and churches of all denominations and individual believers too began to experience harassment, interference from the state and sometimes actual persecution. Tito's regime was far from the horrific atheistic wasteland of Ceausescu's Romania, but few Western visitors to the Adriatic resorts or passing through to Greece realised how much of a police state it actually was. But news of the problems facing Christians circulated among Western churches and there was considerable concern.

So when a Yugoslav travelling through Scotland offered to take literature back into his country when he returned, where it would be distributed among his own people and also taken into other communist countries, the offer was gladly accepted. The need was clear, especially from letters such as this typical response:

> I'm writing to thank you very much for the Bible and the book 'Right with God' which I received quite some time ago. I also wish to apologise most sincerely that I didn't reply much sooner. Because of this delay I feel very embarrassed to ask you if you

> could please send a friend of mine the same, because when I showed her mine she was very interested, so I said that I would send you her address and ask you if you could send her a Bible and the book 'Right with God' by John Blanchard.

There were other contacts with Eastern Europe. A lady in Scotland who had a knowledge of Russian offered to help to produce Christian literature in that language. It would require a typewriter specially modified to print Cyrillic characters. The search began for a suitable machine.

Blythswood's help was requested from even further away. In India, where the Society had contacts in Andrha Pradesh, the region was devastated by freak floods. The local Christians appealed to Lochcarron for help. An appeal was launched for clothing and other practical aid. The Society was moved by the warmth and immediacy of the response, and a quantity of aid was despatched to India.

In Britain, more bookshops were opened; in 1979 it was announced that 'small beginnings' had been made at Inverurie, Lochgilphead, Tain, Dingwall, Londonderry, Tarbert Harris and Scarborough. By 1980 new shops had opened in Oban, Kilmarnock. Workington, Weymouth ... the list goes on. At Lochcarron the staff was enlarged to cope with the increasing workload, not least brought about by the completion of the new extension and the enlarging of book stocks: in 1979 a wholesale department was created.

Jackie's vision for Christian literature was being fulfilled in exciting ways. He always believed that a pastor should see his ministry as extending far beyond the walls of his church, and now out of the tiny village of Lochcarron Christian literature was being sent all over the world. He was being stretched and challenged by the new opportunities, and he was delighted to be given the privilege seeing the work develop.

When at this time he received a call from another church to be their minister, he was forced to think through his situation. Was he really doing God's will in God's place, or simply imagining it because it was such a satisfying task? Was he really open to God's call, to be used in whatever way he could be used? The decision was more difficult because the invitation was an attractive one. It came from the Free Presbyterian Church in the ancient town of Tain on the Cromarty Firth north of Inverness, the site of a great Christian revival in an earlier century but now with a much smaller population. Jackie liked the place, with its old slate and granite buildings and narrow streets, and the Christians in Tain had been very supportive of the Blythswood's work; but after much thought and prayer he decided that Tain was not the place where he should go.

The Society began to look for like-minded organisations with whom they could collaborate in various ways, especially by appointing literature agents in countries; this would simplify and reduce the burden of postage.

The first contacts with the Dutch Reformed Christians in Holland came about for just those reasons. An initial contact came through a minister, Rev. Vergunst, who heard reports of what the Society was doing in Bible distribution, became very enthusiastic about it and raised a substantial amount of support for the Society in Holland. He later accepted a call to a church in Grand Rapids in America. But by the time he left Holland a Dutch Blythswood office had been set up, which handled requests within Holland and also those from Ghana in Africa.

The Bible distribution work in Holland quite quickly became an independent movement of its own. The Lochcarron office had no desire to build an empire, and there were obvious reasons for independence - already some support intended for Holland had ended up in Scotland, which made for increased administrative problems, but more importantly the Dutch wanted a distinctively Dutch organisation tuned to the needs of the Reformed church in their own country. So the two organisations amicably went their separate ways, but the links that had been established between the Society and Holland continued.

The Society also established close links with the Dutch Reformed Seminary in Rotterdam, and these continued to grow. It was in the course of strengthening these links in 1979 that the Society suffered its second major loss when Ian Tallach, the Secretary, died suddenly at the age of 43 from a heart attack, leaving his wife Anne with four young children, aged between eighteen months and twelve years. He was passing through London Airport with Jackie Ross on his way to meet with supporters in Holland.

As well as being a great lover of books, he was also a gifted writer; he wrote a number of tracts for the Society and contributed editorial and writing skills to its magazine. Indeed, his contribution was so substantial that the summer edition of the magazine following his death did not appear: the staff felt unable to fill the gap left by his energy and skill, and it was several months before the magazine appeared again.

In 1980 the Blythswood Tract Society began a collaboration with an organisation that was to become important in the work in a number of ways. It was an Italian organisation called Fede Viva - 'Living Faith'. It was founded by an ex-priest, Franco Maggiotto, who was converted and left the Roman Catholic Church. Franco was a remarkable man, with a sparkling Latin temperament and great personal courage, which was tested to the full in the ministry he was to develop.

He lived for a time in England, where he married Aurora - of Spanish/Italian background - and together they returned to Italy to undertake missionary work at Spotorno on the Italian Riviera. In March 1976 the committee of Fede Viva was established, with two priorities: firstly, translate, publish and distribute Reformed literature in Italian; secondly, to create a centre where priests could come and study the Scriptures with Franco.

John Tallach remembers the tiny flat in Spotorno where Franco and Aurora lived with their toddler daughter Tabitha. He called there once when Aurora's mother, who had been visiting them, was about to leave.

'Let's pray together before you both go,' suggested Franco. Aurora's mother agreed - '*Ma le mie parole saranno poche* (But I won't say much)' she said.

Afterwards John left Spotorno with her. He was travelling on to Tuscany, she to visit her son in a nearby town. As they waited for the same train at Spotorno Railway Station she talked to John about her son. He was a communist. 'If our prayers are not answered before we die,' she commented, 'they will still be there, before God's throne.'

The train arrived, and when they had found seats she said without preamble: 'Now, we do not have much time, so we must talk about the Lord.' The train arrived at her station, and John continued to Genoa, where he sat waiting in the restaurant for his connection to Pisa. 'I was walking on air,' he recalled years later.

> I was still feeling the impact of that simple prayer meeting in the kitchen and that warm fellowship in the train in a country where I had not been used to such things. I have been back to that restaurant frequently, but it has seemed like a different place.

Such simple heart-warming spirituality characterised Franco and his family, and drew many, believers and enquirers alike, to their home.

The movement decided that its new Centre should be at Finale, in Liguria, and in due course bought a building to provide living accommodation for Franco and Aurora and a place for worship. It was a good arrangement, for it gave the small family more living space; also administration was never Franco's strong point and he needed to have a structure around him upon which he could depend.

In September 1980 an agreement was made in Italy between representatives of the two organisations. It was decided the Society would channel financial support to Fede Viva. John Tallach, now a minister in Aberdeen, spoke fluent Italian, knew the family already and was the obvious person to be appointed correspondent. He continued to establish close links with Franco and his family. The financial commitment by the Society and the appointment of

John Tallach amounted to a commitment to support not only the programme of the Italian organisation, but also to support Franco and Aurora, whose second child had by then been born. It was a commitment that was quickly demonstrated when southern Italy was hit by a severe earthquake at the end of the year. A number of Christian groups in America contacted the Society and sent money which was then directed to Fede Viva. As a result the money was passed to a church in the earthquake area where several members of the congregation had lost their lives. There were many more opportunities to help the work, and when in the summer of 1982 Franco and Aurora were able to visit Scotland as part of a European tour, they were able to greet many members of the Society to whom they were considered old friends.

This formal commitment to an international ministry was paralleled at home by a major commercial step forward: the formation of Blythswood Property Holdings Ltd, set up to provide resources for organisations committed to the spread of the Reformed faith, and initially aimed at providing virtually rent-free accommodation for Blythswood bookshops.

A bystander watching the development of the Blythswood Tract Society in the early 1980s would probably have felt able to make some cautious predictions.

Here was an organisation clearly expanding in a very satisfactory manner, with more and more retail outlets and an increasingly heavy demand for the services provided. It had survived the death of two of its most strategic members, Margaret Linden and Ian Tallach; it had left behind its humble beginnings as a student organisation and was now a substantial employer. The Society owned several properties and a number of vehicles, and distributed its magazine to a very wide readership (one small indication of the growth of the Society was that the list of bookshops that usually appeared in its inside front cover now had to be set in smaller type to fit all the new ones in).

Here was an organisation, too, if ever there was one, that was set on a clear path towards an easily-understood goal: the ever-widening influence of Reformed Christian literature through a wide range of outlets, together with the printing and distribution of tracts and related Christian material, and the raising of money for sending free Bibles and correspondence courses to enquirers. The various overseas links were clearly part of an emerging pattern, and the Blythswood Tract Society's course was set full ahead for the immediate future.

The observant bystander could hardly be faulted for drawing such conclusions from the Society's situation. Probably many members of the Society, not unreasonably, drew the same conclusions. The future plan was clear: to work and pray and plan to extend the work that God had clearly blessed so far, and to strive to increase the harvest as much as, in God's will, was possible.

All of which must have caused immense consternation when, in March 1984, a letter was sent to members informing them that the Society had decided to withdraw from all Christian book selling both wholesale and retail, and to dispose of the Blythswood bookshops.

The reasoning, in fact, was logical and sensible. For some time the magazine had carried notices appealing for voluntary help and financial donations to help clear the backlogs that regularly grew up. Often stacks of Bibles, each packed into a labelled jiffy bag and enclosing a personal letter, had to wait on shelves because funds were not available for postage; and shortage of staff often meant that letters went too long unanswered (sometimes even unread).

The letter spelt out the realities of the situation at Lochcarron. One tract distributor whom the Society supplied had written to tell them that he had just distributed his 67,000th tract! As a result of the efforts of such people, hundreds of requests were arriving for free Bibles and correspondence courses. This was, of course, a wonderful result from the tract distribution, but it was placing a terrible strain on the staff and resources. Each enquirer sent back a list of answers to 500 Bible questions, all of which had to be checked and commented upon - dealing with each list took a minimum of eight hours. But there were also the everyday tasks of reading letters, sorting requests, filling out record cards and writing labels for packages.

Nor was there any sign of the task becoming lighter. Every returned question paper bore the name of a person to whom the original recipient had passed his copy of *Let's Study Mark and Acts*. Instructions and answer papers were in turn sent to the new contact. These brought in their turn fresh completed answer papers, each of which meant a further day's work for somebody evaluating it. The staff at Lochcarron and the growing band of volunteer markers were being stretched to the limit. At that very moment, said the letter, many parcels awaited posting and 3,000 letters had been opened but were awaiting attention.

Consequently the difficult decision had been made to withdraw from the Christian book retail trade. The vision for Christian bookshops was still strong, and every effort was being made to hand shops on to local individuals or Christian groups. But in the case of at least five shops, closure was inevitable; they were not self-supporting from their sales, and the Society could no longer afford to subsidise them. Much as it would have wished to, such a decision would have diverted vital resources and finance away from the work of distribution.

For literature distribution, explained Jackie in the letter, was to be the Blythswood Tract Society's priority. That was why the work of itinerant gospel work would go on, and why the book van would remain an important part of the Society's work. The Lochcarron Christian Bookshop, too, would continue to trade, but now under completely separate financial administration from the Society.

It might have seemed, and probably for many did seem, a turning aside from a clear road and a set purpose. The bookshops had taken the name of Blythswood far and wide, and a part of the income from shop sales had funded some of the distribution work.

The need for Christian books was evident in a world where so many were crying out for spiritual values. Was it not a retrograde step, to wind down such a large part of the Society's work?

It might have seemed a failure of nerve. It might have seemed a short-sighted move, motivated by a desire to balance the books (though Margaret Linden, with her firm commitment to avoid embarking on expensive enterprises without money in the bank, would surely have approved).

It might have seemed misguided in many ways. Certainly, it looked like a direction leading them away from the direction that the various small relief projects already undertaken might have indicated, a direction that Blythswood is firmly set in today. But looking back, it was quite simply the most strategic move that could have been made, had those involved known what God was to require of Blythswood in the years to come.

# 5
# The Next Phase

> Please do pray for those receiving their Bibles, many of them now possessing the complete Scriptures for the first time. We, who have had our Bibles for so long, cannot appreciate what it means for these people to have, at last, one of their own. (*The Blythswood Tract Society News and Prayer Letter*, February 1986)

The new situation had its own challenges and frustrations. The decision to close so many bookshops involved administrative and sometimes financial problems; a number of suppliers' accounts had to be met at the same time, and it was only through considerable patience on their part that the cash flow was brought under control again. A sale of stock from closed shops to other Christian bookshops raised some welcome money which also eased the burden.

The extra time and resources now devoted to distribution work were quickly harnessed. Letters were arriving from all over the world. Some came from nurses, soldiers, students and others in temporary accommodation, and often the backlog was such that packages and letters sent to them in reply were sent back to Lochcarron marked 'Gone away'. There was concern that some letters and parcels were not collected and not returned, and were lying neglected somewhere - representing a substantial amount of the Society's funds. Requests also came through other Christian organisations such as the Banner of Truth Trust, the Evangelical Press and the Trinitarian Bible Society. A system was introduced whereby these applications and others were carefully reviewed and a choice made of the most needy people.

But there were encouragements, too ...

In March 1985 the Blythswood Tract Society's stand at the Christian Booksellers Convention in Blackpool attracted considerable interest. The Convention, held in a sea-front hotel, was an annual venue for booksellers all over the British Isles and further afield, who came to inspect displays by publishers and other Christian resource organisations and to attend seminars on subjects ranging from staff training to effective evangelism through literature. For many booksellers, running small shops in outlying areas, it was an opportunity to meet others with the same concern; the Society, with its commitment to the distribution of Christian literature and its recent history of bookshop planting, drew a crowd of interested visitors many of whom were already postal customers. Jackie and his colleagues were enjoying meeting them for the first time.

The African who was making his way towards them, looking with interest at every stand, was of medium height, but his colourful national dress made him stand out among the milling crowds. When he saw the name The Blythswood Tract Society his face lit up with a radiant smile, and he hastened to introduce himself.

He was a Nigerian, a baker by trade, who had read a Blythswood tract in his home town. Intrigued by the offer of further information, he had worked his way through *Let's Study Mark and Acts*, obtained a free Bible and gone on to study everything the Society offered. He had developed a great concern that his countrymen should have the same opportunity to receive the gospel as he had been given, and he decided to spend the profits of his bakery business to achieve this.

'I bought 50,000 tracts from you a few years ago,' he explained, 'and was able to subsidise a really cheap price so that others could buy from me and distribute them. Now they are nearly all gone, and I want to order some more.'

Probably a large part of the increased demand that the Society was receiving from Nigeria was a direct result of that man's work, and it was a great joy for the Blythswood staff to meet him.

One fruit of the many years of friendship and co-operation with the Society's partners in Holland was the arrival, for several summer visits, of Dutch volunteers at Lochcarron, giving invaluable help. At home, a new project had been started: the distribution of the tract *A Word to Ministers* to every minister in the United Kingdom, and some abroad, began on 20 January. It was a huge task; 40,000 names were on the list. As the project got under way, responses from some of the recipients indicated that they had received the tract with appreciation.

Unavoidably, backlogs began to appear. Requests for literature were dealt with in rotation, but the length of time taken to reply depended on the staff available and the finance available at any given time. Although in the previous year 2,500 copies of *Let's Study Mark and Acts* were sent out, this was less than the requests received; by May 1985, some 2,000 copies were awaiting despatch. The urgency of the task and the need to avoid disappointing eager enquirers were very evident, not least from letters such as this from Nigeria:

> When I read over the book *Let's Study Mark & Acts* I ask more questions from the teachers which is not include in the book but I am not satisfy with the answer he gave me. I will now ask you the same question I ask him, the question is -
> 1. Who is the God?
> 2. Who is the creator of God?
> 3. What is the meaning of Believe and Believer?
> 4. How can we obtain Holy Spirit from God?

Financial pressures forced one extremely difficult decision. Each month the Society had been sending the sum of £400 to help Franco's work in Italy. It was a commitment that the Society took very seriously, for it enthusiastically supported the work. But that commitment had been a heavy burden during a time of financial difficulty: in fact, it had resulted in a debt of £2,500. The decision was reluctantly made to inform Franco that circumstances had forced a rethinking. The monthly gift could no longer be fixed at £400; from now on it would depend on the general level of donations received in the preceding month.

It was a difficult decision, and telling Franco was made more so by the fact that Franco's situation was very difficult. A sudden police visit had resulted in intensive questioning in which he was cross-examined about every aspect of his work. The police were polite but insistent, demanding information about the meetings held and the people who attended them. Telephoning John Tallach later he commented that his work had recently been the subject of a good deal of adverse publicity, and he suspected that opponents in the Roman Catholic Church were behind this sudden police interest. He spoke with foreboding of an Italy in which there was little religious freedom and a great deal of fear.

He was understanding, and in fact the contributions were continued at a high level because the level of gift income to the Society remained high. But it was a disturbing foretaste of political pressure on believers in a society which had previously seemed to be free.

The work in Scotland proceeded steadily, if undramatically. Jackie Ross summed up the mood in his newsletter of February 1986:

> We might like to begin our News and Prayer Letter with something exciting - something that would make each one of you sit up and take notice of our news, keeping you in eager anticipation throughout this letter. We don't have that kind of news. Instead, we have to tell you that our work goes on in much the same way as before. Our workers have been occupied in doing what they have been doing for years - reading and attending to requests for God's word and other gospel literature. Unexciting? Tedious? Fruitless? Surely not! What a privilege to be allowed to keep at this work of sending out the Scriptures!

He did have figures to present which, if not dramatic, were a sign that God was continuing to bless the work. There had been a sharp increase in distribution: he presented the figures thus:

| | Oct - Dec | Dec - Jan |
|---|---|---|
| Let's Study Mark & Acts | 1,200 | 2,238 |
| Bibles | 100 | 209 |
| Tracts | 15,000 | 18,000 |

The consequence of such brisk activity was that the backlogs were completely cleared. The figure for tracts referred only to free tracts distributed and did not include the large numbers purchased from the Society by other distributors.

Later in the year the Society was involved in a project that was to foreshadow its later work in an interesting way. Some time before, two pastors from Poland had asked if they could come to Scotland and spend some time with the Society, studying the literature work and also observing church planting operations in Britain. Following their visit, Blythswood sent two trailers; one contained a supply of blankets, food and medicine, the other, Christian literature and building materials. Jackie was shocked by the joy the pastors displayed on receiving the trailers. How could one get so excited simply to receive a trailer for a car? It was such an ordinary item.

It was only when Jackie heard more about the pastors' situation that he realised why they had been so delighted. They and their congregations were working ceaselessly at rebuilding and renovating their churches, but they had no builder's hods or wheelbarrows. It took two men to carry sand and cement, which they did by putting a board on the middle of a ladder and carrying it like a stretcher. A trailer was an unimaginable luxury to them.

Jackie, who had previously thought of car trailers as rather expensive holiday toys, was shaken into a fresh realisation of the need to give help of all kinds.

March 1987 saw a new image for the Society's newsletter. For the past year or so, the old magazine had been replaced by printed sheets, as an economy measure; one by-product of the move was that the older image was left behind, very typical of evangelical literature of the 1950s and 1960s - often with an engraving of a Reformation personality on the front, and using a rather dated letterpress typeface. Now it was decided that to return to a properly printed newsletter was necessary, and much thought was given to producing a format that was colourful, attractive but at the same time serious-minded. The Society was twenty years old, and the anniversary was marked by a number of changes. The title was changed: the *Blythswood Tract Society Newsletter* was now *Blythswood Newsletter*, and the text that had adorned every one of the Society's newsletters since 1974 ('He that winneth souls is wise', Proverbs 11:30) now gave way to another from Revelation: 'The leaves of the tree were for the healing of the nations' (Revelation 22:2). A new logo was designed, a single leaf laid over the word 'Blythswood'. It was a new image for a new world, one different in many ways from the world in which the Society had been formed twenty years before.

The Society had not changed from its original vision, though that vision had broadened and expanded in two decades. The aims of the organisation were set out in that first newsletter of 1987:

> Blythswood has the following aims:
> 1. To give Bibles and Christian literature where possible to anyone who makes request.
> 2. To encourage the study of God's word by correspondence courses.
> 3. To urge others to become involved in the spreading of the Gospel by the use of Christian literature.
> 4. To support Christian outreach by making grants of Bibles and Christian literature.
> 5. To support financially Christian workers in Italy and China.
> 6. To gather and supply clothing and other materials for the use

of charitable agencies and missions at home and abroad.
7. And in any other way according to the doctrinal basis of Blythswood.

The work in China being supported by Blythswood was the Peace Clinic in Hong Kong, where a Scottish husband-and-wife team of doctors - Cameron and Ishbel Tallach - received support from the Society. By comparison with other grants, the contribution was relatively small, but it was an expression of a commitment that was valued by both giver and receiver. Item 6 referred back to previous activities, rather than to any plans for new relief activities. But it was soon to become a priority.

The magazine had the look of a fresh start, though to those in the day-by-day work in Lochcarron and other places there was no sense of a new period dawning. But there were changes afoot. In a country over a thousand miles away, forces of change were stirring. Dissident voices were being raised against a regime that at the time was barely recognised by the West for the monster that it was. Lone voices had spoken out and challenged Western Christians to respond to the needs of their persecuted brothers and sisters, but there was relatively little response. Romania was a closed country, known only for a few legends about vampires and a prodigiously gifted stream of teenage acrobats. Of its orphanages, its ethnic tensions, the progressive destruction of whole cultures and individual freedoms, the West knew nothing. Over the next few years, the West was to discover, to its shame and shock, what lay behind the genial facade of Ceausescu's rule, only recently feted by Western leaders as a brave bastion against the Soviet threat.

But Blythswood, in the providence of God, was by then already deeply committed to the country and its needs.

The first contact had already been made; the man through whom it happened was Jackie's friend, the forceful Strict Baptist who had interrogated him about duty faith on the church steps in 1970.

# 6
# The First Trip

> We must express our thanks for the overwhelming generosity shown in response to our appeal for support for this tour. The enthusiasm and concern shown by so many of you was appreciated, not only by us, but by the Christian brethren in these communist countries. We were encouraged many times throughout the journey by the knowledge that friends at home were upholding us in prayer. This is a constant comfort to God's people in Eastern Europe who are very conscious of the oneness of the Church of Christ. (*Blythswood Newsletter*, April 1988)

'This is Catarina Nagy, Kate for short,' said John Gudgeon, introducing a short, dark-haired young woman whose strikingly clear skin was lit up by a friendly smile. 'She's from Hungary.'

Kate came from Miskolc, a historic town in Northeast Hungary in the hills close to the Czechoslovak border. John had met her parents while visiting Eastern Europe, and had become good friends with them; they were a warm and outgoing Christian family. Kate worked in a travel agency, and when she had mentioned to John that she would like to visit England he had invited her to stay with his family and go to Scotland with them on holiday.

They stayed and talked for a long time. Kate told the Rosses about her home and family and the kind of life that Christians lived in a country that, although superficially in many ways open to the West, was governed by a regime opposed to all religion. She told them, too, of the hardships her friends among the Hungarian community in Romania were experiencing under Ceausescu's harsh regime. Most devastating of all was her account of the

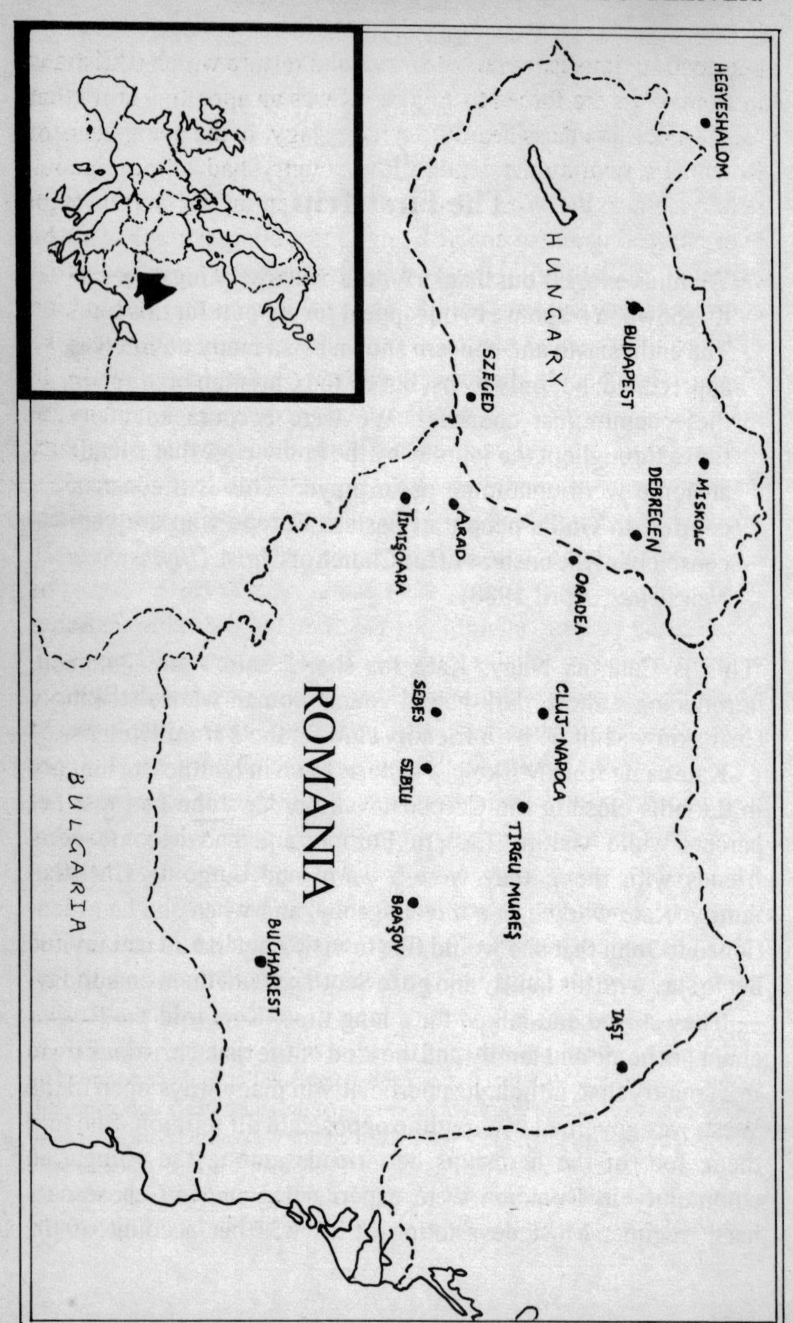
HEGYESHALOM
HUNGARY
BUDAPEST
SZEGED
MISKOLC
DEBRECEN
ARAD
TIMIŞOARA
ORADEA
ROMANIA
CLUJ-NAPOCA
SEBES
SIBIU
TIRGU MUREŞ
BRAŞOV
BUCHAREST
IAŞI
BULGARIA

persecution, imprisonment, beatings and torture which Christians in Romania were forced to endure.[1] It was an appalling story that Jackie and Elma Ross heard from Kate Nagy. In the dying years of Romania's communist regime, the country had an ambiguous relationship to the West. Ceausescu was raping the land through over-harvesting and over-fertilising so that bumper crops could be exported; the struggling fields were dominated by vast industrial complexes, belching out pollution from chimneys that had no kind of filtering or contamination control. In soot-clogged towns like Copsa Mica, people died young of cancers and lung disease. In most Romanian cities, community services were rudimentary; in the harsh winters, old people and babies died because electricity was arbitrarily rationed. Food was scarce. By ruthless overproduction and exporting, Ceausescu had virtually wiped out Romania's national debt, but at a horrific human cost.

The people of Romania were suffering spiritually, too. The constitution guaranteed religious freedom, but the major churches were infiltrated by collaborating servants of the regime. Ceausescu, brilliantly, favoured some religious groups and withheld basic rights from others, knowing that inter-church resentment would inevitably follow. Billy Graham visited the country in 1985, but was poorly briefed by his advisors: his public appreciation for Romania's 'religious freedom' was badly received in a country where thousands of religious leaders had been tortured and imprisoned, and where the church was constantly harassed.

Graham's enthusiasm for what he believed to be the ethnic harmony between Hungarian and Romanian communities in Ro-

---

1. One of the sobering discoveries following the opening up of the Eastern European states has been that tortures and abuses similar to those recorded by people such as Richard Wurmbrand as happening many years ago were still taking place very recently. One who confirmed this was Cornel Iova, the pastor who was to figure large in Blythswood's Romanian trips. His young wife contracted terminal leukaemia, but was refused permission to go to the West for treatment because she would not renounce her faith. She died shortly before the Revolution.

mania was also badly mistaken. For decades, Romanian politics had revolved around the region of Transylvania, comprising two-thirds of the country. Within the living memory of many Romanians the territory had been ceded to Romania by the Great Powers as part of Hungary's reparation for its guilt-by-association in two world wars. By the same settlements Romania lost Bessarabia and Northern Bukovina to the Soviet Union and Southern Dobruja to Bulgaria. Under Ceausescu many Transylvanian Hungarians were forcibly resettled in eastern Romania and ethnic Romanians were moved into Transylvania. Ceausescu's claim to Transylvania argued from the region's status in Roman times, but atrocities on both sides in much more recent times had left a legacy of resentment that still simmered. To this simmering ethnic bitterness could be added frictions with the German community (a remnant from Transylvania's time as part of the Austro-Hungarian empire), the gypsy community, and several other minorities.

At the time Kate Nagy visited the Manse at Lochcarron, Romania was physically impoverished, spiritually oppressed, ethnically divided and ruled by an insane dynasty: Ceausescu - the self-styled 'great hero of the Carpathians' - had already begun his programme of destroying the historic centre of Bucharest, demolishing hundreds of churches, and eradicating entire villages.

Because of Ceausescu's desire to maintain good links with the West (he cherished his honorary citizenship of Disneyland as much as he did the economic support received from America for his Most Favoured Nation status), the West was slow to recognise the terrible truth about Romania. There was no rumour of the secret orphanages that were to scandalise and challenge the West several years later; Romanian citizens themselves did not know such places existed. But the story Kate Nagy told Jackie was of a country on the brink of collapse, of sick people unable to get medicine, families starving for lack of food, and a desperate spiritual hunger that forty years of communism had never been able to satisfy.

In February 1987 it was announced that a friend in Guernsey had offered to provide a camper vehicle for Franco's work in Italy. It was an obvious opportunity to carry out a number of objectives: the vehicle was large enough to carry a substantial load, and an overland route to Italy could be plotted through Hungary, Romania and Yugoslavia - all countries which had been much in the minds of the Society over the years, and now, having heard Kate Nagy's story, a matter of great concern. It was decided that Jackie and his brother Don (who was now minister in the Free Presbyterian Church in Laide, sixty miles from Lochcarron) would drive the vehicle to Italy, and that the trip would now follow an itinerary taking them through Eastern Europe.

In June, Jackie travelled south to Weymouth where he collected the vehicle. He drove it to Harpenden, where John Gudgeon and his wife Margaret helped to pack it full of clothes, shoes, medical supplies, food and literature, which had all been donated by supporters from many places; the van was packed so full that the original plan, that Jackie and Don should sleep in it each night, proved very uncomfortable and was eventually abandoned. Some minor mechanical problems with the van were dealt with at Harpenden, and the Gudgeons gave Jackie last-minute advice on the situations he would encounter in Eastern Europe. Then he drove to Dover, where Don joined him and the expedition began.

Thousands of relief vehicles have made the journey from Britain to Romania since the 1989 revolution, but in those days relatively few made their way across, usually without large organisations behind them, often driven by volunteers. The Rosses travelled as quickly as possible through France, Germany and Austria, eventually arriving at Hegyeshalom at the Hungarian border after two days travel.

Of all the Eastern bloc countries - with the exception only of Yugoslavia - Hungary was the most open to tourists; for decades there had been twice as many tourists in Hungary as Hungarians each summer. Most came from other Eastern European countries, but the low prices and great beauty of the country made it an attractive tourist centre for Westerners too. John Gudgeon had warned them, however, that the border formalities were notorious, and Jackie and Don were apprehensive.

They arrived at the border after dark. The officials approached, their crisp uniforms looking almost military, an effect emphasised by the squat machine guns and pistols that were much in evidence. 'Passport ... Documents ...' A senior official gestured to the Rosses, who handed over their papers. The official grunted and disappeared into an office building. After ten minutes he had still not returned, and Don and Jackie were worried. They got out of the van and stamped the stiffness out of their legs. The cold glare of the few overhead spotlights and the weird stillness of the border post, broken only by occasional vehicles arriving and departing, the voices of the officials and the thick iron bar gate across the road, gave the whole scene the atmosphere of a prison camp.

Another official arrived and requested them to open the van. They hoped he would not demand that everything be unpacked. He looked inside, prodded a few parcels, asked them to open one case and pronounced himself satisfied. Relieved, they locked the van doors again and were delighted to see the first officer coming over with their documents.

They drove towards Budapest along a badly-lit main road, through small villages and anonymous towns. Occasionally the moon broke through the clouds and they caught glimpses of a pleasant, well-tended landscape. But they had not gone far when a policeman stopped them.

'One light not working,' he said aggressively, and demanded an enormous sum of money as a fine. Don got out and inspected the light.

'That's working fine,' he said.

The policeman shook his head and almost shouted: 'You are breaking a law. You must pay.'

'He's just trying to get money out of us,' Don muttered. Jackie agreed. But what could they do, in a strange country faced with a crooked policeman who could barely speak English? Don made a quick decision. 'Here,' he said, and placed a Scottish pound note in the policeman's hand. 'That is enough. Now go away, please.' The risky gamble paid off; the policeman examined the note doubtfully, but waved them on.

Their troubles were not yet over. A few miles further on a brake pipe burst, disabling the brake pedal; they continued with just the hand brake, which caused many tense moments.

The first sight of Budapest was breathtaking, as they swept down from the hills and saw the panorama of the old city ablaze with electric light, its three great bridges spanning the Danube. The castle brooded over the tree-covered heights on the north side of the river, and on the south side the Hungarian Houses of Parliament, a fairy-tale mixture of the London Parliament and a gothic cathedral, was a natural focal point. The red star crowning the central spire was a sobering reminder that this was a country wedded to a Marxist ideology, and the sparsely equipped shops and shabby buildings were a marked contrast to the wealthy cities and trim farms of Austria through which they had just driven.

They negotiated the maze of streets and squares, thronged with early morning traffic - chiefly Eastern European vehicles with inadequate exhaust purification, so that a pall of acrid fumes hung over the roads. Eventually they found a hotel and went to bed early, thankful for the opportunity to sleep in a proper bed after so long on the road. They woke several hours later and explored the city in search of a garage to get the brakes repaired. Their first reaction was that Budapest was not so poor as they had thought; though there was an obvious low standard of living and the shops seemed to have little in stock, the people seemed to be fairly well off.

Searching for a garage brought them sharply into contact with the biggest problem they would encounter in Hungary: the language. Hungarian is a tortuous experience for an English speaker, with its strange accents and unvarying sentence stresses. It is a language in which great literature has been written; the Hungarians are especially fond of poetry, naming streets and squares after some of their great poets. But only Finnish, out of all the European languages, resembles Hungarian, and it is a very faint resemblance at that. Though English is spoken by quite a few Hungarians, one cannot rely on always finding one of them when needed. After some fruitless attempts to explain what they wanted, they decided to go on to Miskolc and ask the Nagy family to direct them to a good garage.

John Gudgeon had warned Jackie that the Nagy home was extremely difficult to locate, but they knew that they would find a warm Christian welcome there. So they pressed on. In the Miskolc town centre they came to a stop - cautiously, because of the brakes - at a set of traffic lights. Around them the traffic was thick and the pavements were full of pedestrians. The two travellers were beginning to despair of finding the way to their destination. But suddenly a familiar face appeared, astonishingly, looking in at the window of the van. Kate Nagy, the one person in Miskolc who knew Jackie, had been out for a stroll during her lunch break and had spotted the vehicle. She guided them to her home where a wonderful welcome awaited them.

Kate's father and brothers offered to repair the brakes. While the work was being done it was discovered that the front axle was fractured and needed extensive welding. The enforced delay while this was carried out proved to be a valuable time for meeting Christian workers. There was also the opportunity to attend church with their hosts, where they met pastors and other church leaders. Some of them had studied in Scotland; Jackie found himself swapping reminiscences of a legendary professor who was known by his students as 'Rabbi Duncan' for his expertise in Hebrew. Some of the Hungarians had heard of him too, and all of them had good memories of Scotland to share.

It was a sobering experience to meet fellow believers who shared their own vision for spreading the word of God, and had pursued it in the difficult and dangerous years of Communism. For Jackie, a highlight was the communion service in which he took communion with the congregation of the local Reformed Church. He was deeply moved by that practical demonstration of the truth that where there is faith in Christ, there is true fellowship: he found himself reflecting on a Bible verse from Paul's letter to the Ephesian Church - Paul was in prison when he wrote it, and he was speaking to another minority church living in a pagan society - 'There is one body and one Spirit - just as you were called to one hope when you were called - one Lord, one faith, one baptism; one God and Father of all, who is over all and through all and in all' (Ephesians 4:4-5).

In Miskolc Don and Jackie found that they had seriously mistaken the level of poverty in the country. Though it was in the middle of a major town, there was no sanitation in the Nagy home. The toilet was a shed in the yard, where a rough seat straddled a deep hole. It was warm weather during their stay, and the hole was permanently buzzing with flies; an unpleasant odour survived the Nagy family's best attempts at cleanliness. Around the shed, a few hens scratched and clucked.

Don and Jackie were struck above all by the generous concern that these Christians had for others; for the poor of their own country, for those in need in Romania, and even further afield. It was all the more impressive because they themselves were far from wealthy. Kate's father in particular made a very great impression on them; a quiet, hard-working man with a cheerful personality, it seemed that there was nothing he would not do for others.

In a few days Don and Jackie saw more new sights and experienced more new experiences than they had ever crammed into a short space before. A man who was familiar from photographs they had been shown by John Gudgeon took them to a gypsy area, which was notoriously dangerous: he, however, was welcomed and treated with great trust and respect, for the gypsy people sensed his commitment to them. Some had become Christians, and there was a friendliness among the community that made the forbidding place almost welcoming.

The friendliness of the Nagy family was in marked contrast, however, to the reception that Jackie had at the local police station. Kate's parents were extremely worried about the delay caused by the car repair, and they stressed that it was a very serious matter in Hungary for a foreigner to stay in a place for longer than he had said he planned to. It would be best, they said, to go to the police now before they come to find you. 'You must explain what has happened.'

At the police station the police seemed unimpressed when Jackie announced that he had come of his own free will to explain that his plans had been unfortunately changed. He was taken into a room with huge double doors and no windows. A woman police inspector gave him what was virtually an interrogation.

'Why have you stayed one day longer here?'

'Our vehicle broke down.'

'Vehicles are easily repaired.' Her eyes were glacial.

'The axle was broken. It was necessary to make lengthy repairs.'

'With whom are you staying?'

'The Nagy family, it is written in our visas.'

The documents were lying on the desk in front of her. Her eyes did not leave Jackie's.

'You will leave Miskolc today, do you understand? You do not have permission to stay longer.' She tapped the passports. 'Today.'

Jackie looked round at the forbidding room, its walls padded from floor to ceiling, the weighty doors pulled shut. 'Today,' he agreed.

He went back to the Nagy's home. He and Don collected their luggage, prayed with their new friends and said goodbye. Soon they were on the road again, the grim police cell a fading memory.

As Jackie and Don travelled further east the landscape began to change, from the gentle hills of Northwest Hungary to the vast flat expanse of the Great Hungarian Plain. A featureless and highly fertile region dotted with small villages and the occasional town, it occupies over half of Hungary. The architecture of the houses was characteristic: small villas set in patches of garden, with neatly kept verges on broad roads, and dominating each settlement the church buildings. They drove through Debrecen, almost at the Romanian border: the ancient city is a heartland of the European Reformation, and the two towers of the Calvin Church and the theological academy behind it form an imposing climax to the breathtakingly broad main street. It is Hungary's second city, and plays such an important part in the Reformation story that it is often called the Calvinist Rome. But they knew nobody in Debrecen, so had no reason to stop there. Soon afterwards they were approaching the Romanian border. The customs post was an ugly complex straddling the long straight road that ran out of Hungary through the flat plain, visible far ahead like a sombre gateway to a fortified castle.

The officials at the border were several degrees colder in their attitude that those at Hegyeshalom. They motioned the van to a side area, demanded the Ross passports and began to search the vehicle. This was the place where Jackie had feared they would encounter problems, and so it turned out; instead of the perfunctory glance that had been given at the Hungarian border, the search was thorough. They were kept waiting for hours, and when the officials finally delivered their verdict it was the worst possible news. A tax of £1,400 had been assessed on the clothing supplies being carried in the van. Unless it was paid, Jackie and Don would not be allowed to enter Romania.

The Rosses explained that this was not a commercial trip but a relief operation, that the goods were to be given away to the poor. But it was impossible to negotiate with the officials. They were adamant. Jackie was not sure whether it was a standard tax or an attempt to obtain a forced bribe; either way, payment was impossible. They did not have the money, and if they had been in a position to pay they would have been very unwilling to do so.

There was nothing for it but to retrace their steps to Miskolc where, after long discussion and prayer a plan was devised. The load would be rearranged, the clothing taken out and the space used for further medical supplies and food. The Nagy family offered to take the clothing into Romania in several small lots over the course of the next twelve months. Jackie agreed willingly and undertook that the Society would pay the costs of the extra trips that the Nagy family would be making. Most of the Christian literature that they had with them was also left at Miskolc, to be distributed as the opportunity arose.

With warm encouragement from the Nagy family they set off again, and found at the border that a different shift of guards was on duty. The new load was passed without problems. They drove across the border and immediately stepped back in time 200 years.

The road surface changed as soon as the border was crossed. Its condition was now appalling - badly metalled, with frequent potholes, and occasionally spanned by unsightly arches of bare pipework. It was impossible to avoid every pothole, and Jackie and Don were thankful that the axle fracture had been spotted in Hungary and repaired. Bedraggled trees lined the roadside, their trunks painted a dirty white for night visibility. Driving in the dark or even the twilight was frightening. There was hardly any street lighting, and at any moment an ox-drawn cart piled high with straw or hay might loom up in front of the vehicle, its driver blissfully oblivious of the large vehicle that was coming behind. The landscape was a flat continuation of the Hungarian plain, but blighted by factory complexes belching out yellow clouds of pollution. The sheer ugliness of the scene was profoundly depressing, and so was the obvious poverty of the houses that lined the street as the van entered Oradea, the most westerly of Romanian cities.

Oradea had once been a splendid town. Its broad streets, fine central buildings and parks were still there, though grossly neglected now. But acres of ugly apartment blocks had been recently built as well, in which the people were regimented in a soulless uniformity that showed in their faces: those they passed on the streets were curious to see a foreign vehicle, but their main expression was one of fear. This was the country where foreigners were forbidden to stay in private homes, where an unauthorised meeting between a Romanian and a Westerner guaranteed several hours of interrogation for the Romanian when the Westerner had left; where Ceausescu's hated Securitate were the most expert and sophisticated secret police in Europe.

In Oradea they booked into a hotel, a drab, gloomy building with little electric light and a great deal of dark panelling. Faded posters advertised holiday resorts on the Black Sea - resorts which only Party officials could afford to visit. The rooms were comfortable, however, and like most Romanian hotels it had a 'dollar shop' at which only Western hard currency could be spent. It was stocked with goods unavailable to ordinary Romanians, but did at least allow tourists to buy presents, though at inflated prices, for their Romanian friends.

They had come to Oradea to visit the pastor of the Second Baptist Church, once pastored by Josif Tson, one of the lone voices calling out to the West in recent years. His visits to England in the 1960s had enraged the Romanian authorities and done much to alert intelligent Christians to the situation in Romania; Tson, for example, wrote an open letter to Ceausescu, arguing that socialism prescribed religious freedoms that were not being permitted in this supposedly ideal socialist state. The church was now pastored by Dr Nicolae Gheorghita and Paul Negrut, both of whom had been brilliant research doctors and had given up prosperous careers to serve God, not without opposition from the state. They were well known among Christians in the West. Neither had any formal theological training, but under their ministry the church was experiencing great blessing from God. It was the fastest-growing congregation in the country. Though the Baptist Church in Romania was affected by pressures both external (the state imposed a limit of 170 pastors) and internal (the use of unlicensed pastors and conflicts between those who wanted to strategically co-operate with the state's regulations, and those who saw their role as pastors as essentially one of opposition), it had a leadership position in the denomination and there were few better able to tell Jackie and Don the facts of church life in Romania.

Though the Oradea church was at the heart of what was a burgeoning spiritual revival, there was terrible material need. Regulations designed to inhibit church growth put limitations on every area of church life, even affecting the number of hymn books available. The Rosses had planned to make their first delivery there, and left supplies of medicine and food. Both were deeply appreciated. Food was scarce and expensive in Romania, and medicine was so expensive that most people given a doctor's prescription could not afford to have it made up. The medicine that had come from England would be distributed among the community.

'Dr Nick' asked them to write a letter when they returned home, to the Romanian Embassy in London and to the authorities in Bucharest, requesting permission for him to leave the country to inspect medical equipment made available through a British charitable trust. They promised to do so. Before they left, they prayed together. As the visitors from Scotland heard Paul's prayer, so full of gratitude for what had been given, they were ashamed. In the privileged West they had affluence and freedom; yet how often they complained and grumbled over nothing!

From Oradea they continued through beautiful countryside, though it was marred constantly by ugly factories and pollution of all kinds. Often acrid smoke from industrial complexes drifted into the cab through the open windows, and in the hills they looked down through wooded valleys to rivers foaming yellow with chemicals. Even the fields seemed tired and drab, the crops stunted and sparse. It was a vivid demonstration of the anti-human philosophy of Ceausescu's regime, which tried to break the spirit of the people by destroying not just their political identity but their ethnic and cultural identity too.

The extreme poverty of the people was obvious in many ways. One trivial example that brought it home to them particularly strongly was the fact that as they drove along in the warm summer afternoon, there was nowhere to buy a cold drink. In the villages and towns, shops were either locked up or had lengthy queues outside. There was no way of telephoning home either: they might just as well have been at the North Pole so far as their families knew.

There were plentiful reminders as they journeyed of the pastoral, gentle way of life of the Romanian people; often in the evening whole families would ride past looking down at them from their perches on top of huge loads of hay, relaxing after the day's hard work in the fields. Others walked, carrying over their shoulders their hand-made hoes and scythes. In the fields bullocks pulled wooden ploughs, and on the roads at night a sudden shape looming dangerously out of the darkness might turn out to be an ox-cart, its driver making his way home without lights. In the villages, old peasant women wearing black carried heavy loads and children played in the streets, often diving away from the van's wheels at the last moment. And as a backdrop to it all lay the undulating hills and dark forests of Transylvania, the name by which Western Romania is better known in the West, though the screen legend of the vampire Count Dracula is a pure fiction and does not resemble the real Transylvania at all.[2]

As the road neared Cluj-Napoca, their next destination, it left the great plain behind and entered the foothills of the central Transylvanian Alps, a dramatic region with roads that dropped vertiginously down mountain passes and round hairpin bends. Safely arrived in Cluj they booked into another depressing hotel, then went to meet the contacts whose names John Gudgeon had given them: two pastors, both of whom had been detained in police

---

2. Nor does it resemble the historical Count Vlad, the fifteenth-century criminal on whom the Dracula legend is based and whose Disneyesque Castle Bran, near Brasov, is a great disappointment to thrill-seekers.

custody; the older had spent several years in prison. They had both suffered police brutality; the younger man had been hauled across a police yard by his hair. Their crime: evangelism.

Jackie and Don's meeting with them was something that the two visitors would never forget. Suffering and persecution had not made them bitter. They were, Jackie was to tell the Society later, two of the gentlest pastors they had ever met. While in Cluj they also met some of the pastors' friends, praying with them and studying the Bible together, with an interpreter helping the visitors.

They stayed in Cluj for a few days, unloading the vehicle there, leaving the food, medicine and literature with a pastor who promised to distribute it among the most needy, as well as the two boxes of clothes they were carrying. They were all too conscious of how little their van had contained and how great were the needs they were seeing, but the obvious delight on the faces of the pastor and his friends was a joy. All too soon it was time to say goodbye. One couple gave them a gift: a small loaf of bread wrapped in a piece of cloth. In a country of severe food shortage and great poverty, it was a deeply moving gift. It might be some time before that couple would be able to eat fresh bread again. As Jackie and Don drove away, the first chapter of James's epistle was much in their minds. The Christians they were leaving were indeed 'perfect and entire, wanting nothing', though they were undergoing trials and persecutions far beyond anything that the two men had envisaged.

The main impression of Romania that Jackie and Don gained was of a country dominated by fear. Especially in the homes of ethnic Romanians, there was a reserve to the welcome; though there was obvious pleasure to see visitors from the West and appreciation of the goods that had been brought, their hosts seemed to be permanently on edge, and it was noticeable that when the visitors left there was a distinct underlying note of relief in their host's farewells. Everyone seemed to be cautious and apprehensive; sometimes they were warned not to speak freely to a particular person, and were left in no doubt that if they ignored the advice their comments would be fed to the security services.

It was a great sadness to be in a country where Christians were under such stress. Even on that first trip the ethnic tensions were very clear; generations of mistrust between Hungarian, Romanian and other ethnic communities had born fruit in church life too. In some cities one denomination had separate congregations for Hungarian and Romanian Christians, even though both shared a common language. The fear was cleverly fuelled by the government and its servant the Securitate, the most hated secret police in Europe. The Securitate kept tight control of individual activities. An example of the controls in force was that if one owned a typewriter, it was compulsory to report not only the fact that the machine was in one's house but also the room in which it was kept and the item of furniture on which it stood.

Anybody who was a Christian preacher or pastor was likely to be the subject of particular harassment by the authorities, especially if the church was active in evangelism or had a thriving youth programme - always a special fear of the Marxist regimes, who knew well that an idea taken up by young people was an idea that would gain power. In one home Jackie and Don visited, background music was played as the group talked in case hidden microphones had been planted to spy on them. 'Yet,' wrote Jackie later, 'these Christians are concerned that others should know about God, and the salvation he has provided. Their own troubles do not distract them from caring for and about those around them.'

The time was now very short and it was necessary to head for Italy as quickly as possible; Don's flight home had been booked from Belgrade. They stopped one night there, but had no time to visit the Christians whom they knew of in the area. The next day Jackie set off for Italy, passing through landscapes of extraordinary beauty and ancient towns and villages to which he was to return several years later in very different circumstances.

Across the Italian border, Jackie stopped for an ice-cream and to telephone home. The two simple acts, so much taken for granted in the West, crystallised for Jackie the impressions he had gained during the trip. Italy was a foreign country - but one could make oneself understood, buy something without queuing, make a phone call without wondering who was listening in without your knowledge. What freedoms the West had! And what a need there was in Eastern Europe, a need that they had barely touched with their small camper full of supplies.

The rendezvous with Franco had been planned at Milan airport. Jackie arrived early and spent some time cleaning the grime of the trip off the van. Then he climbed into the back and slept for several hours, to be woken by a delighted Franco. 'To see Franco's obvious delight when he saw the VW Camper made it a very worthwhile mission,' reported Jackie on his return.

> He so badly needed a vehicle and this one met his needs. There were only 30 minutes to spend with him before it was time to board a plane for London, and then on to Scotland, arriving in Inverness on Saturday afternoon. There was much to be learned from the visit to Eastern Europe. The New Testament imperative of 'bearing one another's burdens' was brought home, and we urge you to consider the plight of brethren under persecution. They value prayer on their behalf, and interest in them from fellow-believers encourages them ... Since the visit, we have sent out literature, worth about £1,000, to over 20 Romanian pastors and students as well as some to Hungary. Literature is allowed in by post, provided it is related to their work. We have been able to send money through a friend to the Hungarian family with whom we stayed in Miskolc. This is to meet their travel to Romania as well as buy food to take with them into Romania. We trust that as funds are provided we will be able to continue to send money to them, as well as to post more books.

None of the Blythswood members knew, reading Jackie's four-page report, just how far the results of this first trip would spread.

# 7
# What Next?

> The one pain above all others endured by Romanians and inhabitants of other Communist countries is not knowing *why* they suffer such pain. (Richard Wurmbrand, *From Torture to Triumph*, 1991)

Back in Lochcarron, the work continued: in April 1988 the Society was able to announce that Christian literature was being sent that month to fourteen countries, including Hungary and Romania. The connection with Miskolc had been consolidated: the following letter is typical.

> I am living far away from theological libraries and the books being near at hand are very helpful for me .... I am a pastor in the Hungarian Reformed Church and spent 29 years in a village near Miskolc. Since 1985 I am a pastor in one of the 14 Reformed Churches in Miskolc.

Another pastor asked for books on Christian education, explaining that theological books were virtually unobtainable in Hungary.

There were frustrations too. When sending books to Eastern Europe, the Society sent them by registered post with a covering letter sent separately. The system did not work every time. One letter received from a student in Romania lamented: 'I am answering your letter sent on 28th January in which you were announcing the sending of several books. I was surprised and thankful, but, no books have gotten to me.' Such problems were followed up as much as possible, but it was very apparent that this was the kind of difficulty that was only to be expected when dealing with Eastern Bloc countries.

The Society moved quickly to send practical help. In Holland, Dutch friends of Blythswood offered to collect food and clothes for the Society's contacts in the Eastern Bloc; the offer was gratefully accepted and various possibilities for delivery were discussed. As in previous summers, Dutch students came to Lochcarron and helped to process over 5,500 requests for Bibles.

A doctor friend, Frank Green and his wife Ruth who were going to Romania as part of their honeymoon offered to take medical supplies with them; money was provided and a good stock of useful supplies purchased. Dr Green turned up to collect them in an elderly sports car which was obviously a much-loved possession, and they packed the medicine in among tent, rucksacks, and other tourist paraphernalia.

Frank and Ruth Green returned with stories similar to those of Jackie and Don Ross:

> We were pretty nervous at the Romanian border and had to unpack the boot of the car twice in quick succession, once for the Hungarians and then for the Romanians. On both occasions we were told to stop before the medicines had been exposed.[1]

The Greens went on to keep in touch with a number of Romanians, and built strong friendships. It was an extremely positive development: it put no burden on the Society, it was a great encouragement to the Romanians involved, and it was a very good experience for the Greens. Blythswood has often encouraged individuals and groups since then to make similar links with Eastern Europeans.

Blythswood people made further trips during the rest of the

---

1. It was during this period, when the Society was taking Bibles into anti-Christian states, that it briefly acquired its nickname 'God's Smugglers', a name originally given to Brother Andrew who for many years - and at great personal risk - smuggled Christian literature through the Iron Curtain. Since the 1989-1990 revolutions, however, the Society has worked through official channels, takes nothing through the borders illegally, and as a matter of principle will not pay bribes at borders nor make use of black market currency exchange.

year, including one that involved the whole Ross family in a memorable holiday expedition.

At Lochcarron Manse, Jackie, Elma and their five children Philip, Sarah, Lois, Jeremy and Jason were making exciting plans.

'Let's do the whole round trip - France, Italy, Yugoslavia, Romania ...'

'Yes! We could visit Franco ... Milan ... Those friends of John Gudgeon ...'

'And we could take all sorts of things to Romania - food, Bibles, books, clothes! We could fill the car up, it would hold quite a lot -'

Once the idea had fired the Ross family's collective imagination, it seemed the most practical and sensible project in the world to embark on a journey that would take them into countries about which Jackie had brought back tales of hostility and danger. What had begun as a plan for a leisurely holiday in the south of France, at a cottage near Aix-en-Provence loaned by a French visitor to Lochcarron, rapidly developed into a major expedition requiring complicated visa applications, hard-to-find road maps and comprehensive first-aid kits. It was summer 1988, and though nobody could quite remember who had first proposed the grand expedition, every member of the family was enthusiastic about it. 'We wanted to meet the people we'd only heard about,' recalls Elma. So the seven Rosses set off for Europe with a great sense of adventure and a heavily loaded car. They took a seven-seater Peugeot, and bought packing cases for the roof rack; inside they carried minimal luggage of their own, and what they did take they planned to leave with friends in Romania.

After a pleasant ten-day holiday in France - an opportunity for Jackie and Elma to take a break from their Blythswood responsibilities and relax for a time - they set off for the Italian border and Franco and Aurora, whom only Jackie had met before. In Yugoslavia, too, where they drove next, the Rosses received a warm welcome; they spent a few hours with a couple whose address had been given them by John Gudgeon: Milan and Brenda Tovarloza. Milan was a Serb who had become a Christian and had come to Britain in the early 1970s. He met Brenda, an Englishwoman from Manchester, at Bible College in Glasgow, and they later trained for missionary work in Watford. In 1988 they were living not far from Zagreb in a town called Moscenica where Milan was working as a mechanic and was also engaged in evangelism; one of the reasons they had come back to Yugoslavia was so that Brenda would be able to learn the language. After that initial meeting Milan and Brenda became a valuable contact for future projects in Yugoslavia.

In France, Italy and Yugoslavia they had driven through some of the most beautiful landscapes in Europe and had enjoyed friendship and hospitality wherever they had gone. Now they turned east from Zagreb and drove through northern Yugoslavia, skirting Hungary's southern border, until they turned north again taking the only road leading into Romania. For Jackie, it was a nightmare revisited; for all of them, the holiday was over and something quite new and frightening lay ahead.

It was almost midnight. A bus was parked in front of the Peugeot in the line of vehicles at the border. The passengers stood in a bored queue waiting resignedly for their turn to be searched. They chatted idly to each other; clearly such delays were an everyday inconvenience. Two customs officials were meticulously checking the bus from wheels to roof. The unfamiliar uniforms, the thoroughness of the officials and the sparse lamplight casting gloomy shadows everywhere gave the border post the air of a military camp. Even in the warm summer night Jackie and Elma shivered slightly, waiting for the officials to turn their attentions to them.

'Passports. *Viza-form.*'

There was no particular hostility in the voice of the young officer, his face shadowed by his peaked cap and the gloom of the badly-lit inspection area. He was simply doing his job. There was no indication of whether he enjoyed it, or whether harassing tourists gave him much pleasure. His face was set in a blank stare of disapproval. He watched as Jackie signed the forms, then vanished with them into a nearby office. Jackie rejoined his family. The same depression he had felt when first crossing the border the previous year was settling on him again.

The inspection of the bus was finished. Its passengers clambered back inside. The officials waved it on. The vehicle roared into life and disappeared in a cloud of dust and noisy vibration. Two of the officials who had been searching it walked over to Jackie's car.

'Open the back.'

The command was tersely polite. The children stared apprehensively at the holstered pistols worn by both men. Jackie was aware that a few feet away a small group of soldiers armed with machine-guns were standing in the murky shadows, watching all that was happening. Jackie studied their faces. *They're terrified*, he reflected. *They're really on edge.* Perhaps the gunmen too were being watched. He nodded to Philip, who opened the back. A bottle of carbonated mineral water, precariously balanced on top of sleeping bags and clothing, toppled over and crashed to the ground. It exploded with a bang that was deafening in the muted, sullen atmosphere.

They did not see the officials draw their guns; the weapons appeared as if by magic. The car was suddenly ringed by gunmen. The machine-guns carried by the watchful bystanders were now trained on Jackie and his family; those who had been searching the vehicle were targeting them with squat pistols, gleaming lethally in the pools of weak lamplight.

The Rosses stared back for a few numbed, unreal seconds. Then one of the Romanians laughed - a relieved, humourless guffaw. The tension dissipated. The officials resumed their search, briefly shamefaced.

'What is in here?'

Jackie described the contents. The officials prodded a few packages. Their manner had relapsed into the same bored superiority as before.

'Everybody out of the car.'

Those who were not already out got out, except for Jason, fast asleep on the back seat; he had not woken even when the bottle exploded. The officials began to search the vehicle. They moved round the outside of the car, thumping the body work; then reached inside and felt the upholstery, lifted the carpeting and pushing bags and other belongings to one side. When they came to where Jason was sleeping they pushed him aside too, roughly, as if he had been a small sack of potatoes.

Eventually the officials finished their inspection and ordered Jackie to repack the car. Their passports and visas were returned. The family took their seats. Jackie started the engine.

Each of them, including nine-year old Jason, was carrying large Thompson Chain-Reference Bibles intended as gifts for Romanian Christians. These Bibles were intended to be left behind in Romania; the family had each memorised a Bible passage. They did so both because they knew they would have no Bibles on the way home, and also because it helped them to understand the situation of Romanian Christians. Many believers only had access to a Bible shared between several families, or owned a few pages from one that had been broken up and shared between the whole church. The officials looked at the Bibles with little interest; tourists were legally allowed to carry one each with them. But Sarah's physics text book, which she had brought with her to revise for a forthcoming school exam, was minutely inspected by several officers who all found it intensely suspicious.

They drove through unlit roads to a hotel in the first city they came to. It announced itself as the Hotel Intercontinental, but the grand title and multi-storey building with its impressive forecourt did nothing to prepare them for the cold rooms, drab decor and primitive facilities inside. In the gloomy lounge, a few people looked with interest as the seven of them waited for their room keys and went through a complicated registration procedure. A few minutes later, in rooms that had no hot water or light bulbs, they climbed between chilly sheets and gratefully fell asleep.

They woke to a view of a city that seemed to be an expanse of concrete apartments and factories. In the early light, huge neon clocks on factory roofs blinked the time and temperature; far below, people were already on their way to work, trudging through the streets or waiting in long queues at tram stops. The Rosses dressed and went down to breakfast.

'If only there was some milk,' said Elma wistfully, putting down her huge mug of cold sugary tea. The others were struggling in disbelief with breakfast: flavourless sliced tomatoes, gristly salami and bread rolls heavy as stones. 'I'm going to ask the waiter,' she decided. But the waiter made it very clear that milk and fresh margarine were expensive luxuries in Romania.

They managed to eat some breakfast and were soon on their way again, heading North-East to Sibiu and on to Tirgu Mures, their destination. In daylight, the city appeared drab and its people, queuing for food at every shop door, depressed and poor. In the centre there were some fine old buildings, but they had obviously been neglected for years. Leaving the outskirts, as the last buildings gave way to fields, there was a huge sense of relief. It was a city that seemed doomed to be forever locked in poverty and fear. As if to emphasise their departure, the city's name appeared on roadside signs to indicate the end of the city boundary: Timisoara, in Banat County.

To their west, the foothills of the Transylvanian Alps rose from the plain, their wooded slopes and tumbling rivers looking stunningly beautiful until one saw the pollution that seemed to reach even the upper slopes. The road to Sibiu had been described in the Romanian guidebook as 'a modern European highway', but it turned out to be worse than a farm track. The surface was so bad that the Peugeot, a large vehicle, had to be driven with great care if catastrophe were to be avoided; but other drivers were a constant problem, especially the ox-carts and horse-drawn vehicles whose huge loads straddled the road.

At Tirgu Mures they looked for the house of their contact, whose name was Ion. John Gudgeon had given them the address, but the house and street numbering system was frustratingly complex; it seemed to be built around dates in Socialist history. After they had booked into their hotel, and gone through the complications of registering again, they set out to find him.

They spent several hours at the apartment, a small unit in one of the grey blocks of flats that covered acres of the town. There was no question of staying overnight there: even had the seven of them been able to crowd into the tiny apartment, it was illegal for a Romanian to provide accommodation for Western visitors unless very special permission had been granted.

'Come in,' said Ion, and gestured to them to enter quickly. He closed the door carefully. They went in to a small living room with simple furniture, and found seats where they could. Introductions followed. Ion was thrilled to meet fellow-Christians, but seemed ill at ease; for the whole of their conversation he appeared to be listening for noises outside. They gave him the presents they had brought, and some luxuries they had bought at the 'dollar shop' in the hotel, which only accepted Western currency and sold almost exclusively to tourists.

There was a knock at the door. Ion looked worried. 'I must ask you to come through here,' he said apologetically, and shepherded them all into the tiny kitchen before going to answer the door. After a few minutes he came back. 'I am sorry, you must stay here. I have a visitor.'

'That's all right,' said Philip politely.

Ion hurriedly put a finger to his lips. 'Please - do not speak so loudly. People will know that I have English people in my home. Please, whisper.'

It was some time before the Rosses were released from the cramped kitchen. The incident illustrated the fear that ordinary Romanians had about talking to Westerners. They themselves were constantly watched by the Securitate, and knew that it was quite possible that somebody in their workplace, their apartment block or even their family was an informer, paid a pittance by the secret police to feed information back to them. When Jackie told Ion that they had brought Bibles for him, a neighbour was summoned who took Jackie outside; the Bibles were handed over in great secrecy some distance from Ion's home, and taken away by car.

They left the goods they had brought from home, and also gave Ion most of their own possessions that they had with them, leaving themselves with only the absolute necessities for the journey back to Scotland. The goods would be distributed among needy people in the town. The depth of poverty in the country shocked them all. Walking in the street in Tirgu Mures they were approached by several Romanians who were fascinated by Jason's clothes. Some stopped to admire them and asked if they could buy the clothes Jason was wearing; but most of the spare clothing they had with them had been given to Ion. When they explained that they could not sell Jason's clothes, some tugged at them as if to pull them off his back. It was a frightening experience, and a dramatic illustration of the desperate plight of the people.

They stayed in Romania for three or four days and left with a love-hate feelings for the country: there was sorrow at having been able to do so little for people in such need, and relief at being able to leave a situation in which they had been constantly afraid that they would cause trouble for Ion and the other Christians.

Sometimes, as friends of Blythswood visited Hungary during that year and talked with Hungarian friends, they speculated about the consequences of certain political moves that were happening in the country. In May the revered leader Janos Kadar, 75 years old, had been ousted from the post of Party Chairman - a nominal position giving the old man great figure-head status. Kadar had played a clever game, balancing his atheistic ideology against the religious demands of the people, but his apparent toleration had masked a strong grip on the religious life of the people. Now he had lost his position unthinkable things were being openly discussed; the possibility of new religious freedoms, of a relaxing of the state's authoritarianism. Who knew where it might lead? The Christians in Hungary watched and prayed.

By November it had become clear that God was moving the Society to expand its activities and commit itself to the physical as well as the spiritual needs of those they were concerned for. But it was going to be expensive, for the literature ministry was expanding too. How could one cut back on a ministry that was operating in areas that had previously been inaccessible? In the Soviet Union, for so long closed to the gospel, the reforms of Mikhail Gorbachev and his programme of Perestroika were beginning to bear fruit. The rigid prohibitions on free distribution of Christian literature and Bibles were relaxed. Bibles could now be sent into the Soviet Union by post. As soon as this was known, an appeal was made for members to send Russian-language Bibles - to be provided by the Society - from their home addresses to individuals in the Soviet Union.

But the needs of suffering people continued to move the Society and its supporters. In November 1988 an appeal was made for funds to pay for specific relief projects; the target was £86,000 by the end of the year. But the Armenian earthquake tragedy in December was a new and unexpected need. Blythswood supporters contributed several loads of clothing and bedding. This was sent to Armenia through the organisations Aid to Armenia and Aid to the Persecuted, including 500 beds and mattresses, and about three pillows for each bed. The bedding came from a work camp on the Kishorn Oil site that had recently closed down five miles from Lochcarron. Two thousand employees had worked there, and bedding and a great quantity of clothing was no longer required, and the owners donated it to the Blythswood appeal.

In the middle of the fund-raising activity, news came to Lochcarron that three portable kidney machines were available at the Edinburgh Royal Infirmary. Would the Society like to have them? Of course the Society would! A telephone call at 12.30 pm got matters moving and by 4 pm the same afternoon the machines were on their way South, on the beginning of their long journey to Armenia, taken by a haulier hired by the Society to a collection depot in the Tilbury Docks from where they would continue their journey by air.

The Society adjusted its target to take the new needs into account. Now they were appealing for £98,900 by the end of March to pay for the projects that had been planned. By January £67,180 had been raised, and the figure was rising.

News of the relief work that the Society was engaging in spread rapidly, and the list of helpers and donors grew rapidly in early 1989: many had been drawn in by the opportunity to help the victims of the Armenian earthquake. Recognising that the Society might be just a name to some who had recently given help, Jackie took the opportunity in an April 1989 newsletter to describe the Lochcarron headquarters.

> It may be that some of you have no idea of the kind of place in which we live and work. The oldest westward monument in the area is the ruin of Strome Castle, the object of many clan feuds in bygone years. The oldest complete and unaltered building on the other boundary of our village is the East Church, built in 1836 to replace an earlier church of 1751 used by Rev Lachlan Mackenzie and Rev Eneas Sage. Along four miles of the sea shore between ... lies the village of Lochcarron with its scattered crofting community. We use the East Church for the storing and sorting of clothes for sending to needy people in different parts of the world ...

He took the opportunity to introduce Blythswood's full-time staff to his readers, too, with photographs and job descriptions: James MacDonald, who was responsible for sending literature to individuals, liaising correspondence courses, and packaging Bibles and other publications; Jessmine MacBeath, who was responsible for processing the initial enquiries; Catriona Oliver, who handled the Russian-Bibles-by-Post scheme; David MacLean, who was 'shared' between the Lochcarron Christian Bookshop (in the same building, but now a separate entity since the decision to split the two aspects of the work back in 1984) and the Society, and looked after the book keeping; and his brother Derek MacLean, who likewise divided his time between the two offices and was learning office procedures. It says something about the closeness of the Blythswood community that the staff of the Lochcarron office is virtually unchanged at the time of writing, three years later.

The Lochcarron Christian Books van had been pressed into service to make three trips in the space of three weeks to Holland, carrying clothes, medicine and literature destined for Armenia. The Dutch had excellent contacts and were able to speed the items rapidly to their destination. Included in the loads from Blythswood were 1,562 Hebrew Old Testaments Scriptures - both Old and New Testaments - and 2,800 booklets entitled Messiah of Israel. These were bilingual in Hebrew and a number of languages and were supplied by the Society for Distributing Hebrew Scriptures. In the East Church at Lochcarron, too, a supply of books was being collected for donation to Logos II, the replacement vessel for Operation Mobilisation's literature ministry run from a ship that had run aground a year earlier.

It is worth detailing these literature projects, if only to emphasise that as the opportunities began to open up for giving humanitarian aid and practical help, the literature distribution was in no way abandoned. Blythswood was not an organisation that started out as a tract-and-Bible movement and changed into something else quite different; it remained committed to the distribution of the word of God and resources for its study, but in an extraordinary way it expanded so that its concern for a world that was lost and suffering spilled over into a commitment to care for physical as much as spiritual needs. It was, after all, different only in scale from the cans of beans and loaves of bread purchased by Society members in the early days and given to the poor and deprived of Glasgow.

# 8
# The Year of Miracles

> My children will grow up and never know there was a Communism ... (Said to the author in early 1990, by a Hungarian Christian businessman)

The 1989 financial statements showed that the level of giving had been maintained, but against the inflationary trend they showed that even more funding was needed if the Society was to fulfil all its targets. The income for the previous years was as follows:

| | |
|---|---|
| 1985 | £87,108 |
| 1986 | £111,431 |
| 1987 | £98,711 |
| 1988 | £98,730 |

Donations from January to May 1989 amounted to £41,000, but to keep up with demands the level of income would have to double. Since 1985 overseas postage rates had increased by over 40 percent, and costs of packaging had also risen steadily, so costs were soaring even before the annual rises in the cost of printing and paper were taken into account.

At the end of the newsletter in which these facts and figures were presented to Blythswood's members, Jackie recalled the very beginnings of the work and the mixed reactions he had had from the churches in Glasgow:

> Years ago when we were discouraged, swamped by work and criticized by others who did not understand our desire to try to

fulfil the need, we were rebuked and spurred on by the following words from Proverbs 24:11,12:

> If thou forbear to deliver them that are drawn unto death, and those that are ready to be slain; if thou sayest, behold we knew it not; doth not he that pondereth the heart consider it? and he that keepeth thy soul, doth not he know it and shall he not render to every man according to his works?

But that was in 1966, and it had been a very different world. Now the call was, to follow the same challenge in a world that was changing so fast that it seemed that the old landmarks were disappearing daily.

It was in Hungary, the first country that Blythswood representatives had formally visited, that the first major cracks appeared in the monolith of the Eastern Bloc, a direct consequence of the new mood in the Kremlin. In May, Janos Kadar lost his last hold on power when he failed to retain his seat in the Party Central Committee. Since his sacking as Chairman the previous year the movements for reform had become more and more vociferous; now the last major obstacle had been removed. A conference was announced, in which, it was confidently predicted, reformers would have a chance to have their say. Later in the month Imre Nagy, the Prime Minister executed in the turbulent events of 1957 when he had argued for what was in effect a second party within the Marxist state, was declared to have been unjustly killed and his trial unlawful. Jackie and his colleagues, and all who had been concerned for religious freedom and human rights in Hungary, watched and listened in awe as the news came through.

It was the first ripple in what was to become a flood of change. In Lochcarron, there were changes too, which deeply affected many who had been involved in the Society from the beginning. The Synod of the Free Presbyterian Church of Scotland, in which Jackie and a number of Blythswood workers were ministers, made the decision to suspend the Lord Chancellor, Lord Mackay of

Clashfern, for attending a Roman Catholic requiem mass. In the aftermath of the decision, a third of the 3,000 members of the church separated from the denomination in protest and formed the Associated Presbyterian Churches. The issue that forced the separation was not directly the Lord Mackay case, which merely brought to a head the underlying issue of liberty of conscience: the right of an individual Christian church member to decide for him or herself, by the light of the Scriptures, what was right and what was wrong.

Among the ministers who signed the Deed of Separation that established the new church was Jackie Ross. Though it was decided he should remain in the Manse, he was now minister of a somewhat smaller congregation. For the first six months they met in the East Church at Lochcarron by permission of the Church of Scotland, but it had no electricity supply and during the cold of mid-winter the new congregation moved to the village hall.

The Lord Mackay story achieved a brief few days' notoriety in the national press. His defence that he had done nothing wrong - that he had not participated in the mass, and that his job as Lord Chancellor required him to pay respect to colleagues who died - and also the Synod's refusal to lift the suspension unless he repented of his action, both appealed to the tabloids' taste for scandal; though the ecclesiastical issues were not discussed and Lord Mackay's gentle and much-respected personality was not mentioned.

For Jackie and his family, and for many like them, it was a deeply distressing time, when relationships were bruised and there were deep hurts. He had trained in the Free Presbyterian Church, and to be at odds with many he respected was hard. But the accelerating events in Eastern Europe were demanding attention too, for doors were opening that had been closed for almost half a century. Letters were arriving from Russians who had received the Bibles sent by Blythswood supporters as far away as Devon and Northern Scotland.

Dear Brothers and Sisters in Christ,
We have received your holy spiritual literature and your letters. Sincere thanks to all those who did not send letters too. The new holy writings and Bibles are God's marvellous bread for man's soul.

Up to a hundred people come to our services in our prayer meeting house. We love our prayer house. We are all pleased and heartened by your wonderful gifts.

Many have asked God with tears of gratitude to watch over you and give you of the treasures of heaven. We will distribute the literature with prayer to the One to whom we are to return.

Christ is risen! Christ is risen! Christ is risen!

If you visit our country, come to visit us. We would be pleased to see you.

The date of the letter was 24 April, and the final blessing in it is an old Russian Easter affirmation. A new Easter, a new resurrection, was dawning in the Eastern European countries.

The early summer was dominated by the crushing of the student protest in Tiananmen Square by the Chinese authorities, seen by many as a viciously bloody answer to the tide of reform that was now running in Europe. In Poland's first free elections for forty years, Solidarity - the first free trade union in the Communist bloc - won a landslide victory over the Communist Party. Mikhail Gorbachev visited West Germany to tumultuous acclaim. In Czechoslovakia an anti-government campaign headed by playwright Vaclav Havel demanded extensive reforms, and in July the deaths of Andrei Gromyko in Moscow and Janos Kadar in Budapest symbolised the changes that were shaking the fabric of the Communist world. By August Poland had elected the first non-communist prime minister in the Soviet bloc and a massive migration of East Germans had begun, taking advantage of Hungary's relaxation of border controls to escape from the repressive regime of Erich Honecker - a migration that Gorbachev implicitly endorsed when he counselled Honecker in October to heed the 'impulses of the times' and institute major reforms.

In the second week of October, Hungarians sat by their televisions in disbelief and watched as the television channels informed them of the Communist Party's voluntary disbanding and the subsequent dismantling in Parliament of the whole apparatus of Party rule. One by one the repressive measures were repealed. Party membership was no longer compulsory. Trade unions were given total freedom. Religious societies in the universities were to be allowed to register. In televised debates and political campaigning, well-known evangelical church leaders were given the opportunity to speak; several later went on to take government and parliamentary positions.

In Germany, huge demonstrations were met by a stony and inflexible Honecker, whose hard-line Marxism had not softened at all. In Romania, Ceausescu was publicly affirming his regime's commitment to Communism and deriding the prophecies of a collapse of the Iron Curtain countries; attempts by Mikhail Gorbachev to direct him towards reform were as unsuccessful as had been the case with Honecker.

But change was unstoppable. On 4 November thousands fled East Germany through Czechoslovakia and one million demonstrators gathered in East Berlin. On 7 November the entire East German government resigned. On 10 November television audiences all over the world saw the ultimate symbol of the Iron Curtain - the Berlin Wall itself - hacked down by the rejoicing German people. On the same day, virtually ignored by the media, Todor Zhikov of Bulgaria - at 78 the longest-serving Communist leader in Europe, having been 35 years in power - was replaced by the Foreign Minister in response to protests and demonstrations in Sofia.

The tide continued to flow. Continuing demonstrations in Sofia, East Germans given freedom to travel abroad without restrictions, a general strike in Czechoslovakia, a summit meeting on December 3 at Malta in which Mikhail Gorbachev and George

Bush officially ended the Cold War, and even a visit to the Pope by the Soviet leader on his way home: still the miracles continued.

The year was not finished yet. In mid-December Nicolae Ceausescu of Romania left Bucharest on a state visit to Iran, declaring his contempt for the reform process and his conviction that his regime would effectively subdue any attempt to repeat the demonstrations that had ousted other governments. While he was away, in an obscure town near the Yugoslav border a Reformed pastor, Laszlo Tokes, defied the Securitate and refused to be evicted from his church. Incredulously, the Rosses listened to the British television news reports of the people storming the police headquarters, of mass uprising against the authorities, of terrible reprisals by the armed forces: 'It appears certain that the Ceausescu dynasty will sleep a little less securely tonight.' The country's borders were closed, but a report from refugees in Yugoslavia spoke to the BBC of 'the whole town rising'.

Tokes' town was Timisoara; it was in Timisoara's Hotel Intercontinental, the Rosses remembered, that they had stayed a year before on their first night in Romania.

The full story only emerged over the next few days. Pastor Tokes's congregation had supported him and publicly demonstrated in the street outside; Romanians of all ethnic backgrounds joined in; the subsequent uprising could not be put down, even by the massacres in Timisoara and in other places. On 22 December a visibly terrified Ceausescu escaped with his wife from an angry crowd outside their palace. Three days later they were recaptured and executed by firing squad, and their sons and daughters imprisoned for trial. The dynasty had fallen. The church bells rang out to celebrate a Christmas that nobody in Romania had dreamed of.

Thousands of miles away in Lochcarron, Jackie Ross wrote a Christmas Day letter to Blythswood supporters.

> They are in need of practical help, now more than ever before. Consequently we are making tentative plans to go to Romania,

> leaving Lochcarron on 15 January to travel in convoy with John Gudgeon and his wife, Margaret, taking with us medicines and medical supplies, specifically requested by doctors. We intend to take as much money as will be available on 15 January. We may take clothes from the supply already collected here. We know that anything we take to our Christian friends there will be put to the best possible use.

For Jackie, too, it was turning out to be a Christmas Day quite unlike anything he had been expecting.

# 9
# Romania Again

> What the Romanian Christians received before the revolution, and what they receive now, is shared with Christians and non-Christians alike. If a benefactor were to visit us with things we needed, would we display the same unselfish generosity? (*Blythswood Newsletter*, April 1990)

The stench was overpowering. Most of it was coming from the single uncovered bucket in the corner of the room that was the only toilet provided. But the beds stank too. The plastic sheets that covered the mattresses were ripped and torn. The children were lying in pools of urine and sodden cloth. The walls had a sheen of damp; mould was growing in some of the darker corners, and patches of exposed brick showed where the plaster had long since fallen away. The brick and plaster dust lay where it had fallen, among the other filth and debris that littered the floor.

'The best room,' announced the guide proudly. The children were sleeping two to a bed, forty of them crammed into the one room. There were no toys, no playthings, nothing brightly coloured or moving. There were no pictures on the walls and no evidence that the children ever did anything but stare, as they were doing now, with large troubled eyes at nothing in particular. Some lay motionless, their limbs at awkward angles, lost in a private world of their own. They all looked disturbingly similar; their hair had been cropped short, giving them an almost bald appearance. The scabs of scurvy on their heads and the skin infections that every child seemed to be suffering from showed that it was probably a crude preventative measure. It obviously hadn't worked very well.

The guide who was showing the Blythswood visitors round

barked an order, and the children dutifully smiled. The visitors could not speak. Most of them were weeping and one driver was choking back bitter fury. Jackie watched him with concern, afraid that he was going to attack the guide who was complacently showing off the orphanage as if it was something to be proud of.

Very few Romanians before the revolution knew the conditions inside the orphanages. Even relatives of the children were rarely allowed inside, and the general public were not permitted to enter at all. Ceausescu had demanded that every woman should bear four children; any woman who did not have the four required by law was immediately suspected of having an abortion, which was illegal; it was not uncommon for infertile women to be forced to submit to degrading interrogation and physical examination. As a result of this policy there were many unwanted children abandoned by their parents and many children who were born seriously handicapped as a result of a botched attempt at a back-street abortion. Both usually ended up in the orphanages, though many should have been admitted into hospitals.

The orphanage was an 'unofficial' one; each region, it was explained, had a state orphanage, but there were many unlicensed ones and many that the state knew of but conveniently forgot to do anything about.

Jackie had been given directions to the orphanage by the pastors of the Oradea Baptist Church, Dr Nicolae Gheorghita and Paul Negrut, with whom they had spent time on their first visit. It was a very different meeting they had had this time.

But then *everything* was different. Romania was euphoric. At the border, the guards who had been hostile and forbidding before were now wreathed in smiles; several flung their arms round the visitors and kissed them. The vehicle had been greeted with cheers as it drove up, and on the road to Oradea every child and adult they passed, seeing the foreign number plate, beamed with happiness and gave the victory sign. Before, the country had been dominated by fear and suspicion. Now there was no sign of the hated Securitate, and visitors were hugged and embraced. It was an extraordinary experience, in this country which had been dominated by fear, to walk down the street arm-in-arm with a Romanian.

The team took 600 bags of clothes to the Oradea Church, for distribution to the community. The leaders of the church there suggested needy places. In the towns and villages to which they went, Jackie and his helpers were appalled by the situations they encountered. They pulled up in one village in the centre of the dirt track that served as main street, causing a commotion among the ducks and chickens that had been scratching for food before they arrived.

It was a village of Hungarians. At first nobody appeared, but gradually the villagers began to emerge from their homes, standing in small groups watching the huge vehicle that had arrived without warning - quite possibly the largest vehicle they had ever seen in their village. For a long time, nobody spoke; they watched in silence as the team undid the rear doors of the lorry, and gasped incredulously when they saw the goods packed inside. They gathered around the lorry eventually, but when the distribution began the villagers were diffident, each standing back to allow others to have the clothes first. Only one woman actually asked outright for something; she needed medicine. She was clearly embarrassed to ask.

There was no reluctance, however, when they asked for Christian literature. 'Do you have Hungarian Bibles? Hungarian Christian books?' they asked, but sadly were disappointed, for the only literature the team had brought was in Romanian or English. Promising to bring more next time, they reflected upon the phenomenon that Christian teams in Romania in those days experienced; the people were more interested in Bibles than in food, and would leave a food queue in which they had been waiting for three hours if somebody nearby started giving out tracts. 'We were reminded of Job's words,' said Jackie on his return. '"I have esteemed the words of his mouth more than my necessary food" ' (Job 23:12).[1]

Back in Scotland, Jackie immediately appealed for help in making a second trip. The cost of the first had been estimated at £25,000, most of which had been spent on goods; the money had almost all been found. The second trip would be from 21 February to 2 March. There was a particular reason for wanting to make the journey quickly.

> From 28 February 1990 a tax is to be imposed on all goods being taken into Romania. This used to be totally unrelated to the value of the goods: e.g. we have been asked for £1,200 for 20 bags of used clothing! ... Consequently we are making plans to return before this tax is imposed, with further necessary supplies and to fulfil specific requests.

He sounded a note of warning which at that stage, in the euphoria of the revolutions of the previous months, might well have seemed unduly pessimistic:

> The opportunities available to us now might not last. Romania's political scene is confused and uncertain. Let us remember what Paul said, 'As we have therefore opportunity let us do good to all men, especially unto them who are of the household of faith.' (Galatians 6:12)

---

1. The trucks were carrying Romanian literature because of the earlier contact with the Oradea church. As Blythswood's work in Romania increased, Bibles and Christian literature in both Hungarian and Romanian were taken in response to requests from ethnic communities. The predominantly Romanian Baptist congregations in Oradea became Blythswood's major focal point in Transylvania, but links with Hungarians in Romania (who were Blythswood's first contacts in the country) have been retained and strengthened too. In a country torn by ethnic tension, Blythswood has never endorsed the political status of any ethnic community group and would support any initiative for reconciliation that was based on a true recognition of individual freedoms and human rights. The same is true of Blythswood's involvement in all the countries in which it operates: it is non-sectarian and its humanitarian aid is given without restriction of race, religion or politics.

Neither the tax nor the reversal of the revolutionary gains happened, but Jackie had correctly forecast the tragically incomplete nature of Romania's revolution. Indeed, observers of the Eastern European situation, noting the ethnic tensions beginning to appear, the unrest in the Soviet republics, and a number of other indicators, were already beginning to predict that the bright hopes of many of the revolutionaries might yet turn sour.

But the doors were wide open for the present. In the three months following the revolution, Blythswood sent six vehicles and eleven helpers to Romania; in July, a further newsletter was issued.

> The initial response to our pleas was wonderful and we were able to take relief supplies to many needy Romanians, both believers and unbelievers. In the six months since the revolution, Blythswood has been able to send in twenty vehicles, all groaning with goods. We are deeply grateful to those of you who made it possible for us to do so, and we give thanks to God for the privilege of sharing in this work.
>
> We would like to do more. We do have two big furniture vans for transporting goods. We do have about three thousand bags of clothing for Romania. We do have volunteers who are willing to do the long haul to take supplies there. However, we do not have sufficient funds to add food, literature and medicines to our load or to cover the expense involved in travelling ... It is usual for donation support to fall after the shock of an initial crisis has passed ... When friends have given generously already this year we feel reluctant to appeal for help. But that reluctance diminishes with a few thoughts of orphanage children in Romania, of women queuing from 7.00 am at the butcher's shop for nothing more than pork fat, of Romanian hospitals where two patients share the same bed. The list could go on ....

It was not only Eastern Europe that needed help. In the Blythswood offices, 9,000 copies of *Let's Study Mark and Acts* had been sent out, but 3,500 packages waited to be sent, 4,000 labels were ready to stick on further packages when literature was available, and 1,000 letters were waiting to be read. They represented 8,500 who were hoping to receive Bibles or Gospels and had individually applied to Blythswood for them. The total cost of sending one copy of *Let's Study Mark and Acts* was £3. 'How good is your 3 times table?' Jackie asked his readers.

Other projects included a major outreach to British prisons, which for several months had been constantly in the news because of riots and confrontations. The previous November the Society had donated copies of *Mark and Acts* to Prison Fellowship Scotland, and by Christmas several completed correspondence courses had arrived from prisoners in Glasgow prisons. Billy Morrison, a prisoner serving a life sentence in Northern Ireland, offered two manuscripts for publication with the topical titles *You Think You are Doing Time Now!* (on the subject of judgement and eternal punishment) and *What is Freedom?* Blythswood was happy to accept them for publication.

1990 also saw the reprinting of nineteen titles. Jackie considered the quantities somewhat disappointing: 'Five thousand each of 21 titles is not really a large number of tracts, not when you consider that almost two years have passed since we reprinted.' He pointed out that whereas the demand from Nigeria for Christian literature was undiminished, there was much less interest from British Christians. Did this, perhaps, help to explain why the eagerness for the Bible was so much greater in Africa than in Britain?

The same resolve not to abandon the Society's existing commitments in the face of the situation in Europe was shown in the note issued in July:

> As we press on with help to Romania and literature to prisons and many corners of the world, we must not forget workers like Franco Maggiotto in Italy and Drs Cameron and Ishbel Tallach in Hong Kong. We may not always be aware of their particular burdens and needs but we know their tasks are not easy. And so we ask you to take them to the Lord in your prayers.

Regular supporters and the general public continued to give generously to support the work. In the period 1 January to 31 July, income totalled £141,320. Because of the needs that were constantly presenting themselves Blythswood relaxed its usually strict rule about not running up a deficit and spent £158,249 in the same period.

A most strategic person in the new developments in Blythswood was somebody who had been involved from the earliest days: Elma Ross. Apart from her support and encouragement for Jackie and the team, and the burden of domestic work which was all the greater because of Jackie's, and other members of the family's, frequent absences abroad, she was a key element in the administration: involved in office work, scheduling, correspondence and a variety of other tasks, and crucially in taking editorial control of the Blythswood newsletters and other publications - the first point of contact, for many, with the organisation.

Over the months, Blythswood was to visit many orphanages and children's homes. One example which was reported to members was visited in July. The team had visited an orphanage at Brincovenesti and had found that they had been given aid already. Like many others they had met, the staff at the Brincovenesti orphanage, rather than seizing the chance to stockpile goods for themselves, asked the convoy to go another orphanage in Tirgu Mures which (they assured them) was in very great need of help. When they arrived they found an institution full of handicapped young people between the ages of six and eighteen years. None were receiving the skilled specialist treatment that their condition required, and the equipment and resources that would have allowed some elementary therapy was completely unobtainable. Yet the children were receiving loving care, given by workers who had nothing but love to give; and the supplies brought by Blythswood were clearly going to be very well used.

That orphanage too directed the visitors to other institutions which, the orphanage staff considered, were in greater need than themselves. The two impressions that all who went on that visit brought back with them were firstly the sadness of a house full of handicapped young people who in the West would have been in specialist hospitals; and secondly, the extraordinary unselfishness and generosity of the Romanian people, who could understandably have taken the opportunity to fill their shelves for months to come, yet were anxious to share their good fortune with others.

Some orphanages had missed the relief convoys entirely. One of them was visited at two o'clock in the morning, when under the direction of a local guide a Blythswood van negotiated bumpy, badly-lit roads and arrived at a building that seemed to be in the middle of nowhere. The shutters were drawn and the high iron gate locked. There was no sign of life inside. But a vigorous banging on the door woke the Director and some of the staff, who came to the windows rubbing their eyes in disbelief. The gates were swung open and the van driven into a courtyard, where the staff delightedly helped to unload the first relief vehicle that had visited them.

The team were taken to the storeroom. As the door was opened they gasped in horror. The room was lined with wooden shelves. There was nothing at all on the shelves. The orphanage housed children of six years old and younger, and there was no food in the storeroom, no clothes, no medicine of any kind. The cupboards were, literally, all bare.

Without further delay the goods were brought in from the van and the shelves began to fill. Basic necessities, bulk supplies of flour and rice, packages and tins, dried food and much more was carried in, but also coffee, dried fruit and other items that are bought casually in Western supermarkets as an afterthought, but in Romania have not been seen in the high street shops for years. The staff were as thrilled with the Christian literature and Bibles that were left with them, and crowded round eagerly as they were handed out.

Romania by September 1990 had lost the first exuberance of the revolution, and anybody in the West who had expected that the execution of the Ceausescus would bring an end to the suffering of the people was by now disillusioned. There had been bitter riots in Tirgu Mures and other Transylvanian cities, where the age-old mistrust between the Hungarian and Romanian communities had flared up into fighting and bloodshed. In March, burnt-out trucks and streets full of broken glass littered Tirgu Mures, a town under curfew and ringed by tanks. A few months later demonstrations in Bucharest were put down by the intervention of miners, and the future of the government of Ion Iliescu's National Front was briefly in doubt.

The initial ecstatic welcome to Western aid at the border had given way to a much less welcoming attitude on the part of many officials, and the paperwork involved had increased markedly. In the first days after the revolution relief convoys had been given free diesel, free hotel accommodation and a number of other concessions; one by one, these facilities were withdrawn. Internationally, the world had competing troubles to deal with and even the most sympathetic organisations were unable to subsidise relief indefinitely; the cross-channel ferry Sally Line, for example, which had made a £10 return fare available to relief organisations, was forced to withdraw it after the first crisis had passed[2], though the company continued to give very generous discounts to relief organisations; and a new term began to gain currency: 'aid fatigue'. With so much need in the world, constantly presented in the media, it was said, people simply ran out of compassion.

There were suspicions being raised, too, about the relief itself and whether it was actually getting to the people who needed it. Stories of surplus food and clothing rotting in Romanian barns began to circulate, and some convoys returned with stories of bandits, looting from vehicles, and organised pilfering conducted by local criminals.

---

2. Were one to calculate the total cost to the Company of the hundreds of subsidised channel crossings it gave, the remarkable scale of Sally Line's contribution to Eastern Europe would be evident. The same can be said of many other organisations that provided discounts and free facilities of various kinds.

There was some basis for this, but it was largely the result of aid being taken in ways that were not always effective. Some vehicles left Britain, for example, with no idea where they were going to deliver their goods. They only knew that they were heading for Romania, because they had seen pictures and heard accounts of the terrible suffering there. They were good and generous people, often sacrificing holidays and their own money to make the trip, and without them many in Romania would have been left cold and hungry. But the lack of contacts meant that some were prime targets for exploitation; some convoys undoubtedly delivered their goods, unknowingly, into the hands of the local black market. Looting, too, was almost unknown among convoys that made arrangements with local people before leaving; but some drivers parked in remote lay-bys on mountain roads and slept overnight in the cab, only to wake in the morning and find that the locks on the rear doors had been skilfully picked in the night and most of the load quietly spirited away.

But Blythswood was able to reassure its supporters that all its deliveries were made to people well known to them, who could be trusted to make sure that the goods would be given to the people for whom they were intended, and that all precautions were taken to ensure the security of the load when parking overnight.

As the year wore on and the poverty of the Romanian people seemed to have barely improved, none of the Blythswood helpers and drivers wanted to leave the remotest possibility that help destined for hungry people might go astray.

'Please excuse my wife's absence,' said the pastor courteously. 'She has gone to buy food for the evening meal.'

Jackie and his companions sat down and tried not to stare too hard at the meagre surroundings; a few pieces of embroidery in the bright scarlet and white colours characteristic of the region, some cherished pieces of pottery given pride of place high on the wall, a shelf of books that were shabby and well-thumbed. The room was scrupulously clean, and the ceramic stove in the corner with its high chimney and elaborately patterned tiles gave out a gentle warmth. The pastor took a few logs from a half-empty box and tossed them inside. Returning to his seat he beamed at his guests. 'She might take a while. Forgive us.'

It was forty minutes before the pastor's wife returned, triumphantly bearing a loaf of bread. The visitors tried to conceal their embarrassment. In Oradea where they had spent the previous three days, bread was unobtainable; long queues had waited for hours at shop windows, only to find that there were only a few dozen loaves to be had and that these were quickly snapped up by those lucky enough to be at the front of the queue. Queuing was a way of life, and most families wasted many hours every week for a handful of shopping. Tirgu Mures, where this pastor lived, was no exception and, being farther from the border in the centre of Transylvania, was much worse off.

The little group shared a meal of bread, strawberry jam and herbal tea, made all the more precious because of the sacrifice that had been made to obtain it. Jackie had no idea what the woman must have paid to have got the loaf in a mere forty minutes; two or three hours was normal. There was no question of declining the food, so that the pastor and his wife could enjoy it on their own. For Romanians of both Hungarian and Romanian communities, hospitality is offered unquestioningly and completely; there is nothing a Romanian family enjoys so much as sharing what they have with others. The opportunity to extend hospitality to Westerners - when before the Revolution a visit from a foreigner guaranteed harassment and possible police action from the state - was one of the most cherished fruits of the Revolution. The worst insult one could make to a Romanian was to refuse the gift of food or drink; many visitors made it unknowingly, out of a reluctance to be a burden to their hosts.

Yet despite the food shortages, much was changing in Romania. Some of the worst abuses of human rights that Ceausescu had inflicted were removed by the Iliescu government; the programme of village systematization was halted, after a relatively small amount of destruction. The revolution had come too late to save the heart of Bucharest, whose ancient streets and picturesque buildings had once earned it the title of 'the Paris of the East'; Ceausescu's ridiculous palace stood on ground razed by the dictator, and open squares in his honour marked the sites where great churches had once stood. But Bucharest had not been totally destroyed. Some districts had been left in their old splendour by the regime for the Party hierarchy, the *nomenklatura*, to occupy and enjoy. After the revolution many of the privileged occupants were put in prison and the buildings given to organisations such as the Romanian-Hungarian Democratic Alliance.

Jackie was especially struck by the scarcity of police. When he had first come to Romania, there were police everywhere; it was impossible to drive for long in a foreign car without being stopped and asked for one's papers. Sometimes the car would be searched; there was always an unpleasant interrogation. Now the police were scarcely to be seen, and road checks hardly ever happened; when they did, the mood was noticeably more friendly. Ironically, this gave Jackie problems when a back wheel axle collapsed as they were driving back from Tirgu Mures in the early hours of the morning with a Romanian pastor. Before the revolution they would already have been stopped at least once by the police; but they had an uninterrupted journey on this occasion and when they needed help, there was nobody to be seen. Two cars had been travelling together, and the occupants got out by the roadside for a conference.

'Let's find a policeman,' suggested Jackie.

A troubled look crossed the pastor's face. 'Maybe that isn't such a good idea,' he said doubtfully.

'They'll know where a mechanic might be found, perhaps,' suggested Jackie, and the other Britishers agreed. The pastor shrugged reluctantly. 'Maybe,' he said.

Eventually they found a policeman, wobbling along the rough

road on an ancient bicycle without lights. Except for the uniform, he might almost have been a British bobby. He showed little surprise at being flagged down by a group of foreigners, and insisted on shaking hands with everybody and introducing himself before finding out what the problem was. When he was shown the car, he took them to a house that was shuttered and dark. 'The mechanic,' he announced cheerfully, and hammered on the door. A sleepy and somewhat irate mechanic agreed to fix the car later in the morning, and went back to bed while Jackie and the pastor squeezed into the second car with the others.

For the visitors, it had been a mild annoyance and a late bedtime. For the pastor, it was a major encouragement, for he had liked the policeman, who could not have been more helpful and friendly. Perhaps it was a pointer to a happier future for Romania, though much mistrust and bitterness had yet to be cleared away on both sides.

It was that trip which decided Blythswood to continue and intensify their efforts to help Romania. They had seen the incomplete nature of the revolution, and had heard many Romanians from all backgrounds express their fear that the revolution had simply raised hopes for nothing and had failed to deliver what it had promised. They had seen, too, that many isolated areas and some major conurbations had not yet received any aid. They had met a number of pastors and church leaders and had seen the disintegrating Bibles and hymn books that were all that Ceausescu had allowed in some of the churches, and had heard numerous appeals for Christian literature and Bibles. Winter was coming too, and the sick and elderly were likely to fall sick. Many would die, some of diseases so easily treated in the West as to be almost trivial.

It seemed that there was no option but to continue with the 5,000-mile trips into the heart of Romania, despite the fact that fuel costs were rising and the weather was worsening. More vehicles were loaned to Blythswood and some donated to the work; three second-hand cars were driven to Romania in the autumn to be given to pastors, after being thoroughly overhauled in Lochcarron.

So the first year of Romania's freedom came to its end. Perhaps easily overlooked amidst the international publicity of events in Eastern Europe, but an excitement to anybody who had supported Blythswood through the years, was the beginning of tract publication in Greek, with translations of two leaflets by the evangelical Bishop Ryle prepared in Athens and sponsored by Blythswood supporters. Their distribution was not limited to Greece; parcels of tracts were sent to Greek seamen all over the world.

Distribution in prisons, too, was going forward, though progress was slow and responses were not as numerous as had been hoped. Efforts continued to achieve wider distribution and to interest prison chaplains in using the literature - some had already indicated their intention to do so.

And as Romania's winter began to tighten its grip, the Society announced in November that two trips were planned before the end of the year, with a forty-foot container loaded with literature and specialist medical supplies as well as the usual goods.

Those who went with Blythswood came back with a variety of impressions. Some were especially moved by the experience of worshipping at the Second Baptist Church in Oradea, which had become a focus for fellowship and encouragement as well as an invaluable source of information and advice as to where aid was most needed. Links with other churches such as the Hungarian Reformed Church were also strong. Two who went in October on a trip to Romania to take aid to both Hungarian and Romanian communities recorded their impressions for the benefit of those who had to stay at home.

Kenneth Macleod, who was one of the car drivers in a convoy of vehicles, recalls: 'Worship at the 2nd Baptist Church in Oradea was a thrilling experience. The church was packed, with the overflow gathered outside. An invitation to stay with members of the church. We talked and had fellowship until 2 am. One who is studying for the ministry asked if we could obtain a copy of the *New Bible Dictionary*. Another, slightly built and frail looking, was in need of 6 months' supply of vitamin tablets which we promised to send on. It was difficult to say goodbye ...'

Calum MacLean was a driver in the same convoy: 'A packed church singing 'O Lamb of God, I come' in Romanian was most impressive. Liviu Costa quietly interpreted the sermon on the healing of the demoniac (Mark 5) which was the preacher's theme.'

Pastor Cornel Iova was a member of the leadership team of the Oradea Baptist churches, and was a much-loved friend of the Rosses and a support and encouragement to many Blythswood teams as they crossed the border and arrived at his church.

A third member of the convoy was Jeremy Ross, then fourteen years old. He recalls the contrast between the visit he had made with his family in 1988 and the situation he found that October:

> It was much different. I don't really know how. In fact there aren't rational ways of describing it except to say that the sun shone when I was there. If it shone in 1988 it didn't really shine. But this time it shone. It wasn't just gloom any more. It was good fun. We could banter with people at the roadside, make jokes with them ... I would go back tomorrow!

Some came back remembering the Christians they had met who had suffered for their faith in ways that they themselves had never imagined. People like Pastor Fulop Denes and his wife Ilova in Tirgu Mures; only some of the many travellers who benefited from their boundless hospitality or made use of Fulop's encyclopaedic knowledge of church life in the area knew that he had been imprisoned for five years for his faith. And many remembered the children, the shaven-headed waifs who had stared at them with large and liquid eyes, sometimes bothered by flies and shifting restlessly in sodden beds; who would often, at the sight of kindly strangers, leap into their arms with cries of 'Daddy! Mummy!'

All who came back had done their share of weeping, but were determined to tell anybody they could about what they had seen.

The anniversary of the Revolution was marked by demonstrations in Bucharest, Timisoara and other major Romanian cities. Anti-Iliescu protests were made but the demonstrations were contained and passed without great violence. In Timisoara, the Hotel Inter-continental was in permanent gloom as delegates gathered from the major Eastern European churches for a conference on ethnic reconciliation hosted by the Hungarian Reformed Church and attended by the Catholic bishop and the Orthodox Metropolitan. Outside in the snow-covered car-park, a skinny little boy pestered the Western visitors for money. One delegate asked at the desk for a light bulb for his room. 'There are no light bulbs in Timisoara,' he was told. Conditions in the hotel had not improved much since the Rosses had stayed there two years earlier.

On 15 December a crowd gathered around the Reformed Church in Timisoara, just as they had gathered twelve months earlier. They held candles, prayed and sang together. Hungarians, Romanians, Germans and gypsies stood together and prayed for unity as pastors from the various Timisoara churches addressed the crowd in turn. Laszlo Tokes, whose courageous stand had provoked the revolution in 1989, took a minor part in the service; he was anxious that it should be truly ecumenical and represent all the ethnic communities of the town.

Later, in the hotel, one by one delegates spoke of the gathering ethnic tensions in their countries. Pastors and priests from the Soviet Union, from Czechoslovakia, from Yugoslavia, Bulgaria and Poland spoke of the coming violence that they feared. 'The Christian church must speak out,' they agreed. 'It is one of the few remaining agencies left in Eastern Europe that possesses any moral credibility at all.'

The one theme stressed by every speaker was the fact of ethnic tension as the overwhelming problem faced by all the countries in the aftermath of Communism. 'The only iron curtain left in Europe,' said one delegate, with rare prophetic insight, 'is the one that separates the ethnic communities.'

# 10
# The Need Continues

As we compile this newsletter the Allied Forces are in the early stages of the Gulf War with Iraq. Changes are bound to occur and we can be sure that those most likely to be affected are those who already suffer hardship. (*Blythswood Newsletter*, February 1991)

December and early 1991 were dominated by the war clouds gathering over the Gulf, and in Britain the armed forces were being prepared for the first major conflict since the Falklands War. The messages coming from Saddam Hussein promised a global conflagration, the 'Mother of Battles', and the apocalyptic language of the invader of Kuwait, the descriptions in every newsreel of the inconceivable power of the weaponry involved, and the very real prospect of massive casualties on both sides, all shifted the attention of the world from Eastern Europe.

In Romania, however, food shortages were more severe than ever. Blythswood teams returning to Lochcarron were reporting that it was impossible to find even bread in the shops, and in midwinter they had seen mothers with babies in their arms queuing for food in the bitter cold at 5.30 am. Husbands and wives queued alternately to allow the husband to go to work, though many work places were operating a short week with consequent loss of pay. A few young people marched in the streets, shouting revolutionary slogans: *Jos Iliescu!* was a common cry - 'Down with Iliescu!' Those shouting it usually marched in small dispirited bands, watched cynically by a few policemen.

'Whatever else Romania needs,' Jackie told the Society's supporters, 'it needs our immediate help with food.'

> Children are hungry. Old people are not receiving the nutrition they require. While we are not faced with the dreadful pictures of starvation that come from the Third World, the food deficiencies, together with the other appalling conditions in Romania's orphanages and hospitals, do cost lives.

It was planned, said Jackie, to send at least three trucks to Romania before the end of January. They would be filled mainly with food, but they would also be carrying farm implements. The new government had implemented its election pledge to return land in individual lots to the rural peasants, but most had no money for tools and seeds. The peasants, Jackie reminded his readers, were in a similar situation to the Highland crofters. Perhaps crofters and other Scottish farmers would like to help? Blythswood had advertised extensively in the press, asking for tractors and trailers and any other power tools; a single tractor could serve a whole village. But anything would be of help, the supporters were assured: saws, scythes, spades, cultivators ... of course, they were able too to collect from England. And room would be found in the trucks for Bibles and Christian books, especially commentaries; these had been requested by pastors and other Christians.

The cost of the trips was estimated at £12,000, but nobody knew whether the Gulf War would drastically affect the price of fuel, and possibly other things as well.

The Blythswood convoy rumbled to a stop eight miles from the Bors customs post on the Hungarian side of the border, for that was where the queue started. A long line of parked cars disappeared into the distance, their occupants sitting on the verge or wandering fretfully around. Occasional fights broke out and there were many voices raised in anger. Almost all the cars were Romanian. The drivers had taken what money they could scrape together and gone into Hungary in search of things that were unobtainable at home. An eight-mile queue was normal at Bors; it was the nearest border crossing to Oradea.

A Western car went past, but its driver reversed to tell the convoy that Western vehicles were expected to go directly to the head of the queue. Thankfully the vehicles started off again, accompanied by angry shouts from those in the cars ahead. Some tried to attack the convoy, but could not keep up with it. They had been waiting, Jackie calculated, at least eighteen hours. When the Blythswood vehicles reached the customs post, bored officials processed their passports and visas and waved them through; they did not even have to go up to the main visa office, now always crowded with Romanian tourists returning and having their baggage meticulously searched. Within minutes they were on their way to Bucharest.

This was a December trip; for the first time Jackie's nineteen-year old son, Philip, was a member of the team. It had a number of objectives. The first stop was Oradea, where Pastor Cornel Iova welcomed them with comfortable beds and an invitation for Jackie to preach at the Fourth Baptist Church. The Baptists of Oradea were experiencing, not for the first time, a period of great growth and blessing, and the foundation stone had already been laid for a new church building which was to be the largest Baptist church in Europe - itself a symbol of the extraordinary history of the past few years. The situation of the people, however, was desperate. As the team unloaded food at the church for distribution in the community, Philip carried in a crate of oranges which seemed to be particularly appreciated. Intrigued, he asked Cornel: 'How difficult is it to get oranges in Romania?'

'It is not difficult,' said Cornel wryly. 'It is impossible.'

Philip's first sight of the queues at shops and petrol stations, and his realisation of the fact that in Romania people were deprived of fruit which in the West we regard as a casual snack, moved him deeply. At the service at the Fourth Baptist Church, Jackie preached and Philip and Donald MacVicar, a third driver, were asked to give greetings to the congregation from Scotland. Deeply moved by the joyfulness of the congregation and their radiant spirituality in the face of so much hardship, Philip told them: 'I've travelled 4,000 kilometres to get here, I was feeling exhausted and I wanted to be back at home. But now I have met you, I would travel 8,000 kilometres to be with you ...'

In Sibiu, a computer was delivered to the home of Anca, a young lady who was to translate Christian books into Romanian, and large quantities of food and clothing were left there for later distribution as well. They arrived at her house at two o'clock in the morning, and were invited to stay the night. Next day they set off for Bucharest. The long majestic range of the Fagaras mountains, capped in white, loomed over the bleak snowbound landscape, but the drivers were too intent on negotiating the narrow icy roads to look much at the scenery.

The original plan had been that in Bucharest, medical supplies would be transferred from one of the Blythswood vehicles to another lorry that would meet them there. But when they arrived in Bucharest the lorry was nowhere to be seen and a frustrating wait followed. During this time Philip explored the Palace, still damaged by the fires during the revolution. It was a profoundly depressing experience. The Palace is approached from the huge Boulevard that Ceausescu intended should eclipse every great street in Europe. It is lined by shops, and has the superficial look of any European capital. It is only when one looks at the shop windows and sees the prices high above any ordinary Romanian's pocket, or goes inside the Palace and sees the shoddy workmanship, grandiose design and arrogance of the architecture, that one realises how completely it sums up the waste and destructiveness of the regime that ruled the country for so long. The Palace is empty now, and nobody wants to have anything to do with its 7,000 rooms. A book is kept there for visitors to sign. It asks for suggestions: What would you like to see this building used for? But nobody has come up with a convincing idea.

'Bad news,' announced Donald MacVicar as Philip arrived back at the truck. 'The other lorry didn't wait. They've gone on to Timisoara.'

'How long do you think it will take us to get there?'

'About four, maybe five hours.'

They looked at a map. 'It means going through the mountains,' said Jackie. 'And the weather's getting worse.'

'We don't have any choice,' said Donald.

'We've got to meet up in Timisoara. Anyway, it's on our way home ...'

At nine o'clock they left Bucharest. Snowflakes swirled down, weakly illuminated in the few street lamps. Soon they were on the open road, the street lights left far behind, ploughing through a deepening slush, the windscreen wipers pushing thick snow from the screen. Drifts made driving dangerous, for the surface was poor and there were numerous concealed rocks, some the size of a small car.

'We're running low on diesel,' said Philip, pointing to an indicator gauge hovering near the empty mark. But there were no petrol stations for miles, and before they could find one the tank ran dry. It happened twice, and both times they were forced to leave the vehicle and look for diesel on foot. By 4.30 in the morning they were approaching Sibiu, hours later than planned, and it was decided to wake Anca and ask if they could spend the rest of the night at her house. Next day, with full fuel tanks, they set off again for Timisoara. On the way they stopped to take a photograph of two mountain shepherds clad in ankle-length sheepskin coats and fur hats. They gave them fruit and tins of fruit: it was a sobering experience to see the shepherds kissing the tins in joy.

The old town in which the revolution had begun looked cold and miserable, its acres of bleak apartment blocks and chilly squares drab and shrivelled in the winter sunshine, the locations of the massacres marked by wooden memorials round which red candles guttered in the icy wind. The news at the meeting-point was bad again. Half the load had to be taken to Sebes, another two hours away on the road to Oradea. There was nothing for it but to set off again. Finding the way was a nightmare; there were hardly any signposts, and at one point two very drunk soldiers insisted, when asked for directions, on coming into the cab and directing them - it rapidly became obvious that they were being taken in totally the wrong direction. They finally arrived in Sebes at 3.30 am and by 4 am the lorry had been completely unloaded. In the middle of the unloading, Philip was astonished to see a woman on her way to the shops to queue for food.

Back in Oradea they relaxed at Cornel Iova's home before leaving for the final haul to Scotland. Cornel spoke longingly of Romania's need for tractors, to work the ground that had been given back to the people. Some had been given by Blythswood; more would be wonderful. 'If you will drive me a tractor all the way from Scotland,' he assured Philip with a twinkle in his eye, 'I will find you a nice Romanian wife.'

Philip had seen many attractive young Romanian ladies on the trip, but after a total of 200 hours of driving, mainly in treacherous and hostile weather, he decided that for the present he was content to remain a bachelor.

Later Cornel wrote a note of appreciation to Blythswood's supporters:

> We want to thank you very much for your help for Romania: clothes, food, cars, tractors. We appreciate very much your effort, and your feelings with Romania. These demonstrate that you are real Christians, and you feel with your brothers from Romania. We are the same family, the best family from the earth, the family of God. God bless your families. We pray for the wonderful people of Scotland to know all of them the love of God.
>
> Now in Romania is winter, and winter is not like in Scotland, here is cold (-15° to -20°) all is frozen and a lot of snow. We appreciate very much your kindness, and we love you all.
>
> By your help you felt with a lot of families which are obligated to stay in long queues for milk, bread, petrol; and they have not meat, oranges, good clothes. All the money which you invested in the things for Romania are not lost, you borrowed from God, and you will receive back in heaven. God bless you, and a lot of greetings from Romania.

In April, Cornel was able to deliver his greetings in person. He visited Scotland and spoke in ten different places about his work as a pastor in Romania, and was able to meet many of the people who had contributed to the aid that had been sent. He made a great impression on those who met him for the first time. 'The earnestness of his preaching conveyed how much he cared about souls being saved,' wrote one young Christian who heard him in Dundee. 'The people in Romania seem to be gasping for the gospel. We, I think, should take a lesson from them.'

Trips were made throughout 1991. 'When we hear desperate cries for help we are confronted with a difficult decision,' reflected Jackie in May. 'Whom should we help first? Africans, Romanians Russians, Kurds and many more are in great and urgent need. Christians should be the vanguard in attending to the spiritual and physical needs of their fellow men ...'

Blythswood was forming effective links with other organisations active in Eastern Europe. Somebody who was a valued advisor and encourager was Bill Scott, who has worked for years among the Reformed churches of Eastern Europe. At an early stage of Blythswood's overseas relief work he told Jackie, 'If I can do it - you can do it!' Bill later joined the council of Eastern Europe For Christ, a council made up of Reformed churches. As the author can testify, having met Bill Scott several times in Romania, the work of EEFC and the council has been a source of spiritual encouragement and practical support to many Eastern Europeans for years.

Some people who were friends and members of Blythswood asked the Society for advice on where to take goods (advice which Blythswood is very willing to give to anybody who requests it). One such person was a surgeon from Orkney, Bill Groundwater. Bill arrived at Lochcarron the day after Jackie had received a letter from Iasi in the Moldavia region of Romania telling of a hospital that was in great need; Blythswood teams had visited the town the previous autumn to deliver seed and agricultural aid (on that occasion an Englishman, Mark Shiperlee from Worthing, acted as advisor to Blythswood; he had been deeply challenged by the agricultural needs of Romania, and was committed to arranging distribution and sowing programmes).

Bill had come to ask where in Romania he might most usefully deliver a load of medical supplies. Jackie gratefully directed him to Iasi. On his return, Bill wrote a report for Blythswood. The details of the physical dilapidation and poverty were familiar, but the medical facts spelt out, in the clinical sparse language of the professional, made chilling reading.

> This hospital caters for very young children with severe infections or malnutrition. There are over 100 beds and many of them are occupied by children infected by the AIDS virus, approximately 25% of them with overt AIDS syndrome are doomed to die. Of those currently in the hospital and with remediable conditions, many have been abandoned by their parents and will eventually be transferred to an orphanage for long-term care .... All medical and nursing materials are either non-existent or present only sporadically and in quite inadequate quantities. Much of Romania's problem with AIDS in children is the result of transmitting infection by the repeated use of syringes and needles, a practice which is unknown in the West .... Overall this hospital seemed to me to present a situation not seen in the UK since the turn of the century.

Reports such as these circulated widely in Scotland and further afield, for the Blythswood address list was expanding all the time. The Society's response was swift. Six trucks left Lochcarron, three to deliver medical supplies and other needs to Iasi, three to take food, clothing and agricultural equipment to other parts of the country. One driver, Graham MacSween, took his wife with him as helper; other helpers, some experienced and some going for the first time, joined the convoy to help with the driving and unloading at the destination. Such rapid reaction to a plea for help was made possible not by any great skills of Blythswood but by the generosity of their supporters. The continuing plight of the Romanian people was touching thousands of hearts, so much so that the East Church in Lochcarron was bursting at the seams with aid arriving daily. Space was so scarce that the vehicles parked outside were packed with unsorted aid, but that solved nothing as there was nowhere to take the goods for sorting.

In early June, Radio Highland, a station which had publicised the work of Blythswood among Romania's poor, announced the problem on a news programme. A few hours later an offer came from Dingwall, a town near Inverness. A large building, until recently used as a bus garage, was available if wanted, rent-free from Ross and Cromarty District Council. Did Blythswood have a use for it?

When Jackie inspected the premises he was delighted. It was a large open space with some basic office accommodation, with enough access to allow the Blythswood vehicles - by now a small fleet - to be brought indoors for loading. There was ample space for storing and more importantly sorting food, clothing, literature and medical supplies, and the location was near to several towns in which willing volunteers lived who would have been unable to make the journey to Lochcarron. As a further bonus, four large inspection pits would make it possible to carry out maintenance work on the vehicles.

Jackie gave thanks and accepted the offer immediately. He sent out a newsletter informing the supporters of the new expansion. It contained a reminder from Philip that the work of sending out Bibles and literature from Lochcarron was continuing.

> It is difficult to find news about the work of sorting and sending out one hundred requests for Bibles every day, day after day. Nevertheless, this work is in many ways more important than the work of feeding the hungry and clothing the poor and is equally worthy of your prayers and support.

This did not mean that the Blythswood commitment to practical care was diminished at all. On the contrary, Philip urged further efforts.

> Journalists may have become bored with Romania. Most of the orphanages have been helped and every newspaper, radio station and TV channel has joined a convoy of lorries. The fact is the poor are still poor. However the prayers of many poor people in Romania have been answered, through your help. In May a lady in Deva told one of our helpers how in March she had a problem with finding clothes for her children. She prayed to God to help her with what to most of us is never a problem at all. A few days later our lorries arrived and out of the thousands of bags and boxes she was given clothes for her children. Though others may easily forget, we urge you not to forget. Please help us to help others.

With the new facilities, and greatly increased giving from the general public, it seemed that everything was in place to make the summer programme of trips and projects run more smoothly than ever before.

But that was before Jackie's second newsletter, arriving days after the first, brought terrible news of what had happened to the convoys.

> We did not intend sending you another newsletter so soon. However, something totally unexpected and tragic happened on 24 June ...

# 11
# Tragedy in Romania

They were always trying to help others.
(*Daily Record,* 27 June 1991)

The roads to Cluj in the mountains of northern Transylvania are steep and badly surfaced, with hairpin bends and inadequate signposting; a common sight is a broken-down cart, with a fallen horse or an ox that has wandered into a ditch. For a motor vehicle the descent is often terrifying, as the wheels slip on the loosely gritted road and the valley far below appears frighteningly in view without protective railings to intervene. At about 1.45 pm on Monday 24 June, four Blythswood lorries were making a slow precarious progress down a difficult hill when Graham MacSween's vehicle went out of control, left the road and plunged into a deep, partly-wooded valley. The other vehicles stopped and their shocked drivers and passengers gathered at the edge of the precipice. Below, in a cloud of oily smoke and swirling dust, half buried in the fresh earth gouged up in its headlong slide down the mountain, the parts of the truck lay like a dismembered body. The main container section had been smashed apart as if made of balsa wood. The cab was twisted at a grotesque angle, the steel and glass bent and shattered. Separate from the rest of the wreck the trailer platform lay upside down, its wheels pointing towards the sky. Bags of clothing and other items from the load were scattered all around, among broken fragments of the truck.

There was a stunned silence, punctuated far below by occasional rending scrapes and small avalanches as the tortured metal and loosened soil fell back into position. Then a frenzy of activity began. Some rushed for help, others clambered down to the wrecked lorry. They found Graham conscious, but trapped in the cab. His wife Fran had been thrown out of the cab by the impact, and when she was found she was obviously too badly wounded to be moved without help.

For an hour the team waited for an ambulance to arrive. In the wrecked cab, Graham talked to the others as they attempted to free him, but it was soon clear that he could not be freed without special equipment. Fran drifted in and out of unconsciousness. Both were in severe shock. The ambulance finally arrived, but it broke down on the way back to the hospital in Cluj. The journey took an hour and a half. Fran's condition became critical. When they arrived at the hospital it was found that the driver had made a mistake and Fran should have been taken to a different hospital; another delay.

Fran died shortly after finally arriving at the right hospital. An emergency operation was being set up, but it was too late. Besides damage to limbs there had been massive internal bleeding. The long journey to the hospital had made the situation much worse.

Back at the site of the accident, the rest of the team had no knowledge of the tragedy happening in Cluj. There were no emergency services with metal cutters available, no equivalent of the British Fire Service which turns out in minutes to such accidents with sophisticated rescue equipment. Local people who had rushed to the scene collected hacksaws from their homes and slowly and painfully cut the cab into pieces. Eventually it was possible to pull it apart by towing with one of the other trucks. The whole process took six hours. During the frantic sawing and pulling, Graham remained conscious, directing the rescue operation in the cab with considerable courage.

He was taken to hospital in Cluj with a shattered ankle and badly damaged arm. The rest of the team were taken care of in friends' homes in Cluj.

Jackie and Philip Ross and Donald Campbell, a driver who had made several trips to Romania already, had gone on ahead of the convoy by car to Iasi to make arrangements for unloading the convoy. They arrived at four o'clock; the convoy was expected at eight. When eight o'clock came and went they were not unduly alarmed - delays were not uncommon, and drivers often took longer than expected to reach their destination. They drove back towards Cluj for about an hour looking for them, but decided to turn back; either the convoy had stopped for the night, or they had missed the trucks in the dark and they were already in Iasi. By midnight, however, they had heard nothing from Cluj and were by now extremely worried. They tried to telephone through the night, but could not get through. In the morning, desperate for information, Philip telephoned Cornel Iova in Oradea to see if he had any news of the convoy. Cornel broke the news to him of the accident and Fran's death.

They returned immediately to Cluj and went straight to the hospital. Graham's condition had worsened. A massive infection was spreading through his body. The doctors greeted Jackie with a grim prognosis. 'His life is in great danger,' they said. 'We must perform an immediate amputation of the leg. There is no other way to halt the infection.' Jackie persuaded them not to make an immediate decision; he wanted to seek advice. 'But there is not much time,' the doctors warned. When Jackie saw Graham in his ward he realised the seriousness of the situation. It was an isolation ward, with two beds; a woman with advanced terminal cancer lay in the other. It was impossible to maintain a sterile situation; the hospital possessed neither the resources nor the staff to do so.

He found the team stunned and confused. They did not know what to do next; nobody wanted to move from Cluj and the police had asked them not to go far away. The long wait for the ambulance to arrive and the sequence of catastrophes that had followed had shocked them, and Fran's death and Graham's serious injury could not but cause the others to fear for their own safety.

A Scottish policeman on the team telephoned Lochcarron and broke the news to Catriona. Fran's next of kin had already been told of her death by Graham's cousin Neil, who was also a member of the team. Catriona's main concern was to tell relatives of the other team members what had happened, to avoid unnecessary worry and speculation as the news began to spread. All day, and for most of the evening, there were constant telephone calls on the office and Manse lines. That evening the story appeared in the television news and later in the newspapers. People prayed in homes and churches all over Britain. One Free Church of Scotland Presbytery heard of the tragedy while in the middle of their regular business meeting. They stopped their discussions immediately and turned to prayer for the team.

In Cluj, decisions had to made quickly. The team, distraught and disorientated though they were, prayed together and discussed the situation with Jackie. A group decision was made. They would do what Graham and Fran would have wanted, what they had left Scotland and come to Romania to do. They would go to Iasi and deliver the load. The hospital equipment, vital medical supplies, food and clothes which Graham and Fran had helped to pack and had driven across Europe must finish their journey. The wrecked lorry's load was retrieved - though much of it had been looted during the night - and distributed between the other three vehicles. The convoy restarted its journey East, accompanied by Philip and Donald. Jackie remained in Cluj, where Graham's condition was causing the gravest concern.

Major surgery in a Romanian hospital, handicapped by lack of resources and with no guarantee of the skill or the cleanliness of the surgeons, was unthinkable. Jackie knew that if the operation went ahead it might well introduce infection rather than contain it, and Graham's chances of surviving would be minimal. In any case, there was no way of knowing whether the diagnosis was correct. It might be that a needless operation would leave a young man handicapped for life. Jackie began to search for the 'wide-spectrum' antibiotics that would help; there were none on the trucks and in Romania they were scarce. He and a Red Cross worker frantically raced round Cluj, knocking at the door of every contact that might have some. For much of the time he was running alone through the streets of the town, praying out loud: 'Help me, Lord - help me!'

Other Christian organisations working in the region had by now heard of the accident and were offering help and comfort. Operation Mobilisation's 'Love Europe' workers based in Oradea were just some of those who joined in the search. Finally a small quantity was found and rushed to the hospital, where a dose was administered to Graham immediately.

'The infection is being held back,' said the doctor cautiously. But he looked worried. 'It may begin to spread again. This is a very bad infection. The antibiotic will not last for long.' Everybody knew that only a temporary respite had been achieved. If Graham had to stay in Romania he was certain to lose his arm - more, he could easily die. Jackie found a telephone and spoke to certain friends of Blythswood. Would it be possible to raise a guarantee against payment of chartering an air ambulance? The arrangements were made. These too were frantic, as no air company would agree to carry both a body and a seriously ill passenger. Prices, too, were prohibitive - around £30,000. Eventually some of the Mackenzies and their staff at Geanies House located Heathrow Air Ambulance who chartered a company from Bonn and a plane was booked to take Graham direct from Cluj to Glasgow, a journey of three hours.

Donald and Philip, having seen the load safely delivered at Iasi, drove back by car to Cluj. As they approached the hospital they heard the wailing siren of the ambulance taking Graham to the airport where Jackie was meeting the plane. They followed. As a final horrific twist to the tragedy, a Romanian airport official almost refused to allow the coffin to be put on the plane, and was only persuaded to permit it after a bitterly angry protest from the German pilot and a frantic phone call by Jackie and the pilot to the British and German embassies. Jackie, Donald and Graham's cousin Neil left on the same plane, and nineteen-year old Philip, emotionally drained and physically exhausted, was left in Cluj to deal with a few remaining matters. He was looked after by a sympathetic Red Cross worker and drove back to England a few days later just in time to attend Fran's funeral.

She was twenty-seven years old. The couple had two children, aged six and four.

In all such tragedies, the commonest question is 'Why has God allowed this to happen?' Wisely, Blythswood, in informing their supporters of the tragedy, did not attempt to look for silver linings or take the opportunity to expound a doctrine of suffering. It was, Jackie acknowledged, a mystery, part of God's 'eternal purpose' and in some incomprehensible way part of his glory. 'We trust him,' he wrote. 'We know he will never leave or forsake us in grief and in difficulties.'

There was certainly an element of miracle in Graham's recovery. British ambulance teams are trained to free trapped limbs in the fastest possible time, for they are taught that a crushed limb trapped for four hours or longer will certainly have to be amputated. Graham's foot was trapped for six hours, which made the massive infection inevitable, but the fact that he still drives trucks into Romania with functioning legs (one is still weak, and he walks with a limp) defies rational medical predictions. But there were even more significant indications that God's providence was involved even in tragedy.

Looking back on the accident from a distance of over a year, the Blythswood leadership do point to a number of ways on which the tragedy was used by God to deepen and refine the work and the understanding of those involved. It was a time, for example, when any in the team who might have been tempted to rely on the expertise and efficiency that Blythswood had developed, and to see the relief aspect of its work largely as a human organisation with worthwhile humanitarian aims and considerable skill and experience, were forced to realise that the Director of the operation was not man but God. In a situation of fear and danger, when tragedy and despair were raging, many in the team found fresh courage and commitment as they prayed together in Cluj. It was a time, too, when many found that what they had known about intellectually and affirmed as doctrinal truth actually worked; it could be tested in human experience; the love of God and the fellowship of the Holy Spirit were not just words but facts.

It deepened, too, the commitment of many people to Blythswood. The story of the tragedy and the bereaved family resulted in an immediate cash influx as supporters made their contribution to the £15,000 charter fee that had been paid for the air ambulance and the numerous additional expenses that had been incurred. But though the money was necessary and appreciated, even more important was the number of people whose prayer commitment and practical help increased. The Society had never wanted to build a support base of purely financial backers. A praying family, with understanding of the issues and the needs, was what had always been sought. The tragedy in Romania enlarged and challenged that family.

And perhaps the most challenging result of the tragedy, in view of Blythswood's future activities, was that it brought home to them in a unique way what it was that they were doing in Romania in the first place. It was one thing to take medical supplies to a hospital, spend a day there and return to Scotland to collect more medicine. It was quite another matter to have a colleague lying in one of those rough beds, to know that your friend would probably die because there were no antibiotics to be found, to watch the coffin of a young woman being loaded into a plane and wonder what would have happened had the ambulance been on time and had not broken down on the way to hospital. In a very real way, and a way that nobody would willingly have chosen, Blythswood had indeed suffered as the Romanians suffered. As Jackie struggled with the bureaucracy at the airport and dealt with the complicated procedures for taking a human body by air, as he searched the basement mortuary and had to cope with the distress of identifying Fran, and as he counselled and prayed with the members of the team still in Romania, he experienced an intensifying of his own commitment and recognised the same thing happening in his colleagues.

In Glasgow the surgeons praised their Romanian counterparts for the work done on Graham's arm and leg. Taking into account the limited resources, the hospital had done an excellent repair. But everybody knew that had the antibiotics and money not been found, certain amputation and probable death would have been inevitable.

The rest of the team returned safely from Iasi, but they too had a story to tell. When they had arrived a crowd of about three hundred had surrounded the convoy and tried to break the doors of one of the lorries open. When the team had succeeded in unloading the supplies at the hospital they left, hoping that the crowds would disperse; but an attempt was made to break into the hospital to seize the goods - which were, to all intents and purposes, useless to them, as most of the load had been specialised medical supplies. The only solution was to call the police, who duly arrived armed with menacing Kalashnikov rifles. When they saw the guns, the crowd finally broke up.

Later, one of the trucks disappeared for four hours - it was being detained at a PECO station by a dispute over the value of the pound. This caused further worry to the team. Eventually at half-past midnight Philip had to set out in his car to look for the truck, accompanied by a soldier with his Kalashnikov, the Iasi Police Chief and the local Army Chief. In Iasi a policeman stopped the car; the Police Chief gave him a bruising dressing down at astonishing volume.

Over the next months the MacSween family - Graham, little Graham and Debbie - became the subject of much care and prayer as Graham fought back to health and the children began to adjust to a new life. Blythswood supporters were kept in touch with their progress. In October, Jackie wrote:

> Often when tragedy occurs in someone's life, such as happened to Graham, they will become bitter against God and man. It is a

joy for us to see that the effect on Graham seems to have been just the opposite.

The work of Blythswood continued. In Romania, the Society appointed a translator, Gabi Damien, to work on literature projects and also to help with distribution of aid; it was a major step forward to have a permanent representative in the country, not only translating books such as John Blanchard's *Right With God* but also helping to supervise the distribution of aid brought by the Society. The existing literature ministry to other countries was struggling. The financial burden of the accident had meant a drastic curtailing of the mailings; by October, 14,300 copies of *Let's Study Mark and Acts* were packed, labelled and waiting to be posted. Two thousand Bibles and a variety of other literature were also awaiting funds to enable them to be sent to their destination. Requests for free tracts from many sources were likewise awaiting funds so that the literature could be sent. A minimum of £15,125 was needed to get the work going again.

A Blythswood van that had been used for a number of trips was donated to a friend of the Society, Tom Ross, an Irishman who had been living in Romania for several years. His ministry was to the gypsy community, which in Romania is despised by a majority of the population. Often associated with the Hungarian community, and sharing their unpopularity, the gypsies of Romania are a very needy group. Some church planting has been done among them, and there are gypsy pastors, but sadly gypsies are not welcomed in most Romanian churches; their reputation for pilfering makes them mistrusted.

There are many tragic sights in the gypsy villages. Jackie in his visits often saw girls who could not have been more than fourteen years old, with two children. Incest was common, and promiscuity. Yet he often observed a deep, instinctive spirituality among them; such as on the occasion when he came upon a gypsy encampment where somebody was dying inside one of the huts. Around the building was gathered a group of sombre, silent men and women, clearly profoundly moved by the fact of death. 'Yet these were the same people,' he commented later, 'who would half kill each other in a fight and afterwards stitch the wounds crudely and treat the whole thing as if it were nothing.'

There are a number of Western Christians working among the gypsies who have reported encouraging responses to the gospel and families and communities being touched and transformed by the love of Christ. Tom Ross's projects were for both the physical and the spiritual needs of this ethnic minority; the Blythswood van would be a great help to him. In a letter to Jackie he movingly described the work in which he was involved.

> For quite a while now I have been spending most of my time working in Oradea prison and with the prisoners' families. This work has led us to a people at the very bottom of the social ladder. The places where many of the prisoners' families live are almost untouched by the rest of Romanian society. It is not possible to describe how terrible the conditions are that some people live in ...
>
> There is also a lot of sickness. We visit one home and try to help the family. When we first went there we found a twenty year old girl naked and tied at the wrists to a post in the dirt floor. She is mentally ill as is her brother, her mother and her father. Other families let their children run naked in summer and then try to get them something to wear for the winter. Recently we went with shoes to a family with fifteen children all of whom had no shoes. It had been snowing and they were running around barefoot.
>
> People in the West are very much moved by scenes from the orphanages. THE CHILDREN IN THE ORPHANAGES COME FROM THE HOMES WE WORK IN. We want to help BEFORE the children are put into orphanages.
>
> I could write much about the suffering but we do see results. We see families finding hope and most importantly we see people trusting the Lord Jesus Christ as their Saviour.

Further trips to Romania included one to an orphanage in Arad for which equipment had been provided by friends of the Society living in Aberdeen. A forty-foot articulated lorry driven by two Inverness men, Keith and David, left Inverness on 4 October, bound for an orphanage in Arad where Caring For Life, an English organisation based in Leeds, was transforming the building. In Arad they asked directions from a local man who took them to premises where they were welcomed and given refreshment. Conversation was curiously stilted and many of the questions Keith and David asked were met with blank incomprehension; it was only after they had enjoyed the staff's hospitality for several hours that they realised that they were, in fact, sitting in the wrong orphanage.

The discovery was accepted philosophically by their accidental hosts, and Keith and David later reported that this orphanage needed aid too. They parted on friendly terms and soon afterwards were pulling up at their original destination. Voluntary helpers from Aberdeen were there to greet the Blythswood visitors and help unload the complete kitchen they had brought.

The bureaucracy appeared to be increasing. David and Keith reported that the border crossing had been much more difficult than they had expected; apparently some aid convoys had been abusing the aid concessions and the authorities were taking a tough line. In Arad, once the kitchen was unloaded the remainder of the contents of the van had to be itemised under the scrutiny of the Customs Department in the town. Then they drove north to Oradea, where they met Tom Ross. The rest of their load was for the gypsy community.

The two Scotsmen were shaken by what they saw of gypsy living conditions, the drab legacy of discrimination under Ceausescu's regime. They saw houses made from mud bricks, through which rats had gnawed their way in; all along the walls were large rat holes. Larger holes in some houses, Tom explained, were because some gypsies sell bricks from their houses because they are so poor. Some sell half the roof and live under the other half. Many live in huts with turf roofs, the gaping holes in their walls stuffed with whatever rubbish might keep out the cold.

Besides the Romania trips, new ventures were announced. A truck loaded with food, clothing, toiletries and medicines was sent to Poland, to the Jewish centre in Warsaw. Part of the load was food, destined for Jews emigrating from the Chernobyl area. News was only now beginning to reach the West about the dreadful conditions in the region; the after-effects of the reactor catastrophe had sent economic repercussions into thousands of homes, and the scale of the poverty and other problems was only now beginning to become clear. But the Jews of Chernobyl were leaving for other reasons too; anti-Semitism was active in the region.

Jackie was unsure what the reaction of the Jewish community would be to receiving aid from an organisation so clearly part of the Christian church, but was assured by a Jewish Christian friend that the help would be accepted with gratitude. It has always been Blythswood's policy to give, as resources permit, to those in need without distinction of race or religion; for did not Jesus Christ himself heal and feed and care for the deprived and disadvantaged whoever they might be?

The greatest gift that Blythswood considered itself able to give anybody was the word of God, so over the years many Bibles and Christian publications have been given to Jewish communities and individuals. But it was never a condition for giving help. The same is true of the vast majority of Christian relief organisations in the needy areas of the world; which is a marked contrast to the behaviour of, for example, some Western cults presently operating Eastern Europe who have promised to rebuild orphanages in return for a wholesale embracing of their beliefs.

In late 1991, Blythswood began to look towards Albania, the last closed country in Europe. Contacts with the Albanian Evangelical Trust and remarkable co-operation from the Albanian government made the decision a logical one, especially as reports were arriving of terrible suffering in the country on a scale nobody had expected to find.

# 12
# Into Albania

*Hitch-hiking in the Communist countries: Albania.*
Forget it.
(Ken Welsh, *Hitch-Hiker's Guide to Europe*, 1971)

The nurse in the hospital grounds was hacking at branches of a tree with a small axe. She was scavenging for wood to light a fire to heat water. The job was difficult; the only branches left were high up so she had to stand on tiptoe and reach high off the ground. All the lower branches had been broken off already. Once the tree had obviously stood in a garden. There were the remnants of a path that might have been well-cared for, and a few straggling stumps of shrubs that were all that remained of a hedge. The woman stopped chopping eventually, and gathered her sparse gleanings together. When she had gone back indoors a man appeared from one of the adjoining houses and cautiously approached the spot. Rapidly he picked up the small chips and fragments of wood that the nurse had left behind. Pleased with his handful he went back to his home.

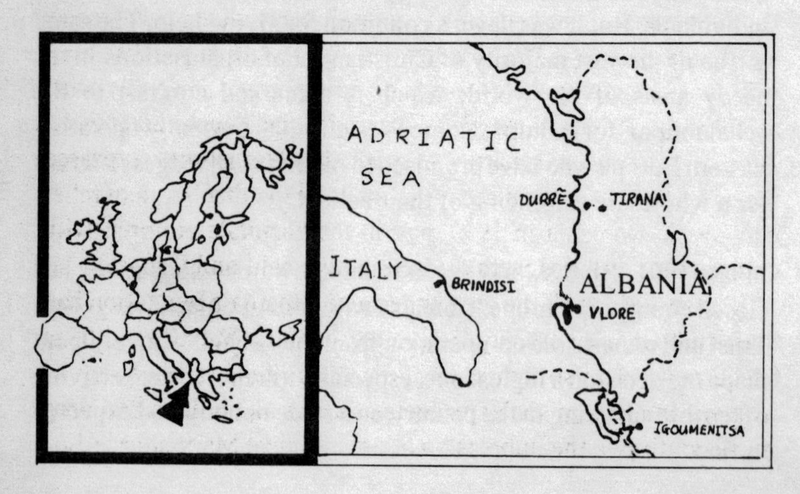

Albania is a country that seems, to the Western visitor, almost destitute of wood. Buildings are in poor condition, with gaping holes and broken windows that cannot be mended. The people have felled olive groves and vineyards for firewood, and tracts of empty land are all that remain of farmland that once provided food and work for the community. When the country became open again after decades of secrecy, the horror of the West at discovering the appalling social conditions, poverty and suffering was matched only by the Albanian people's disillusionment at discovering that they did not, as their great leader Enver Hoxha had assured them they did, enjoy the highest standard of living in Europe.

The problem that confronted organisations like Blythswood on first coming to Albania was a complex one. Of all the Eastern European countries, Albania had the worst infrastructure and the most primitive economic structures. It seemed that Hoxha's vision for his country had not matched that of Tito in Yugoslavia, for example, whose five-year plan in the 1950s at least secured economic and agricultural progress. The roads were in poor condition, the telephone system ineffective; medical infrastructures in particular were hardly developed. In the hospitals and clinics the sanitary facilities, the water supply, the linen and other basic services were all hardly workable. The beds in which patients lay were poorly made, and the decoration and standard of cleanliness were so bad that those who had encountered Romanian orphanages and hospitals were appalled to see how much worse their Albanian counterparts were: Albanian orphanages in particular recalled and sometimes surpassed the worst horrors of the discoveries made by the first Western relief convoys to Romania in 1990, and in the hospitals children with chronic skin diseases were dressed in rags held on by rope.

The shock was all the greater because Albania's reputation had been that of a rigorously controlled country but one with an adequate welfare structure. Reports of its literacy, liberation of women, and lack of social problems such as alcoholism and drug abuse confirmed the impression of a puritanical Marxist hard-line state, run as it was by the longest-surviving Communist leader in Eastern Europe; it was assumed by many observers that the people were not fat, but not starving either. At Hoxha's death in 1985, preceded by a stroke in 1983 which forced his withdrawal from public life, his successor Ramiz Alia recognised that modern radio communications and the impossibility of maintaining a completely closed border and highly controlled tourist industry meant that Hoxha's puritanical Marxist isolationism could not survive. This was especially so in the face of unrest within the country and worsening relations with Yugoslavia over the disputed territory of Kosovo, many of whose Albanian inhabitants were claimed to want to secede from Yugoslavia and return to Albania. Hoxha had considered the Kosovo region a potential corruption of his state, and the possibility of an influx of seceded Kosovars was a worrying prospect for Alia. At the 1988 first Balkan Conference Albania was represented - a huge step forward for a country in which watching Yugoslav, Greek or Italian television had been an offence for which one could go to prison.

Albania was notorious as the only country in the world that had outlawed Christianity. Countries like Romania, in theory at least, possessed religious freedom; that had, in fact, been the argument put forward by Josif Tson in his famous open letter to Ceausescu in the 1970s: that socialism ought to honour its own commitment to freedom of religious belief. Although, as the world knows, there was consistent and destructive pressure put upon religious believers of all kinds by Ceausescu (except when for cynical reasons he favoured a particular group, either to foment inter-church resentment or - as in the case of his favourable treatment of the Jewish community - to secure preferential treatment from the West), the constitution of the country permitted freedom of belief. In Albania, however, even this nominal safeguard did not exist. Its believers were persecuted more ferociously and more secretly than in any other European country.

The first contact of any kind that Blythswood had with Albania was at the time of the Romanian revolution, through the Albanian Evangelical Trust. At that time the country was closed to relief vehicles. Tourists were allowed in but there were heavy restrictions: the visit had to be arranged through the recognised tour operator. If a visitor strayed from the official route and investigated on his or her own, they would be firmly redirected to where they were supposed to be. As in several other Eastern European countries, in pre-Revolutionary Albania one saw what one was allowed to see and no more. There was no chance at all of entering the country as a private tourist or driving a relief van. But even the official tours showed much of the country's poverty. A friend returning from Albania remarked to Jackie, 'By comparison, Romania feels like a Western democracy ...'

One story in particular illustrates the kind of country that Albania became under Hoxha. Mother Teresa of Calcutta was born of Albanian parents, though her birthplace was Skopje, in those days part of Serbia.[1] Her work in Calcutta caring for 'the poorest of the poor' has brought her the admiration and affection of millions. After she had gone to India, her mother and her sister went to live in Tirana the capital city of Albania, where her brother years before had taken a commission in the Albanian army. In 1970, she returned to Yugoslavia for the first time in 42 years, where she was warmly welcomed by the Socialist government and her work was endorsed by the authorities in Skopje. Two years later she received an urgent letter from her sister, saying that her mother, who was extremely ill, was asking for her. Mother Teresa immediately began a long and humiliating attempt to be allowed to see her dying mother, but entry to Albania was consistently refused. In Rome she applied to the Albanian Embassy, but the officials would not speak to her. Indira Gandhi and U Thant of the United Nations both attempted to intervene, but it was useless. Her mother died in Tirana without ever seeing her daughter again.

It is a powerful symbol of the entrenched isolationism of Enver

---

1. At the time of writing it is the capital of Macedonia.

Hoxha and his extreme government that the best-known and most distinguished humanitarian in the entire world was not permitted a visa which had been requested on compassionate grounds.

But now it was 1991: Enver Hoxha was long gone and the winds of change had blown even into his fortress state on the Adriatic. 'Two Blythswood vehicles are at the time of writing en route to Albania,' Jackie announced in November.

> Between them they carry 4 tonnes of food, one tonne of medical supplies and half a tonne of clothes and bedding. They are travelling to Italy, making the sea journey to Greece and then proceeding to Albania. They are to be met at the border by Ministry of Health officials who will escort the vehicles to their destinations. The drivers are Donald MacPhail and Donald Campbell from Stornoway, Hans de Visser from Holland and Philip Ross from Lochcarron. From them we expect to glean information on how best to proceed with future help to Albania. Our hope is to be able to supply Christian literature to evangelicals there. We understand that conditions are generally worse than in Romania and the lawlessness that prevails makes relief trips hazardous. We are thankful to have the co-operation of the Albanian authorities on this occasion.

Even with the co-operation of the authorities, the inadequate infrastructures of Albania made the simplest relief operations complicated. Tractors, for example, were in great demand and over the next months Blythswood took several to Albania. But tractors need fuel, and fuel was in short supply. So the Albanians requested Blythswood to send only tractors that consumed less than a gallon of diesel a day - an impossible request. The problem that the farmers faced was therefore twofold; how to obtain tractors (which Blythswood could help with) and how to obtain diesel (which they could not). The distances involved, and the need to create facilities for distributing fuel in areas where no diesel distribution structure had existed previously, was a dramatic illustration of the creaking infrastructures and the scale of the task of rebuilding its economy.

Blythswood has also been asked to provide ambulances for outlying rural areas. But what use is an ambulance in a country where the roads in such areas are dirt tracks, so rough that a Land Rover would not be able to easily negotiate them? Many women who have complications in childbirth die before they get to a hospital, but the answer is not better vehicles but better roads.

The first trips into Albania carried clothes, food, medicines, dental equipment, Bibles and New Testaments. The load was organised by the Albanian Children's Relief Fund, which was linked to the Albanian Evangelical Trust with whom Blythswood already had contact. The plight of Albania's children was already attracting concern and compassion, and once again supporters of Blythswood gave generously, both those who were regular givers and those who knew little about Blythswood but were moved by what they had seen on television and wanted to help.

Travelling inside the country was, as Jackie had feared, hazardous. Once through the border the country is bleak, with dry and dusty roads that are narrow and only partially, if at all, metalled. For the Blythswood convoys with their double-axled vehicles driving was exhausting, as both wheels rarely had tarmac beneath them at the same time; trailers in particular were a problem. The most direct route is through the mountains, which are dramatic, rocky outcrops with sparse vegetation, not unlike the landscapes of Northern Africa. But the condition of the roads is not the only reason that drivers have little time to watch the scenery roll by.

The main danger on the roads is that of interference from bandits and thieves. When first obtaining information about the country from others who had already been there, Jackie was warned to stop as infrequently as possible. 'Don't even stop for police,' he was once told. 'There have been cases of police stopping the first vehicle in a convoy while their colleagues robbed the last one in the line.' The advice came from an Albanian police escort that was guiding them to a hospital.

Being last in a convoy was a known danger; if that vehicle is attacked there is nobody coming along behind to help, and it may be difficult for those ahead to come back. Once a vehicle has stopped it becomes vulnerable to a whole range of skilful pilfering; convoys have had lights stolen, items unscrewed, and even cables cut and taken away by thieves who are able to dart beneath the vehicle and out again before anybody notices. Sometimes the Blythswood vehicles were stoned in an attempt to ambush them for their loads. The best time to travel in Albania, they quickly decided, was four o'clock in the morning when most people were asleep.

The overwhelming poverty of the country is plain everywhere. In Romania, the villages often conceal their poverty to Western eyes because of the apparently idyllic pastoral scenes of ducks and cattle, ox-carts, and breath-takingly beautiful scenery - all extremely attractive to those who do not have to live there. In Bucharest the absurd folly of the Palace and the surviving beauty of the remaining winding streets and old buildings that Ceausescu spared give the city a superficial elegance - again, few are able to enjoy it, and for the rest it is a prison of poverty. But in Albania there is nothing to please the eye, no pastoral scenes or European cityscapes. The country seemed to Jackie like a vast gypsy encampment. He noticed that the houses, like Romanian houses, had big metal gates that were kept locked; but unlike Romania, here there was almost always somebody - probably a family member - on guard outside every home. There was an abiding feeling of mistrust among the population, and a willingness to steal from neighbours, which shocked the visitors and made them realise again the gulf between the prosperity of the West and the poverty of such countries as Albania. There are no grand buildings, no formal city squares: there is nothing in Tirana to make you realise that you are in the capital city.

For children, begging is a way of life, and scavenging too when the opportunity presents itself. Once, after a street distribution, team members were finding it hard to close the vehicle doors.

Though people were leaning hard against them, something was resisting them. When they stopped, the door flew open and a small child leaped out. He had crawled inside to help himself and had become thoroughly alarmed when he heard the engine start up. He raced off empty-handed.

The team thought it was highly amusing; in such a country, it is hard to think badly of people who steal when they have so little, and stealing requires some ingenuity - relief trucks when distributing are guarded by armed police to prevent pilfering. 'I know of people who have slept in their vehicles and woken up to find their tanks drained,' Jackie recalls. 'But then you can always get enough diesel to get you to the next place, just by pleading with the next relief vehicle ...' He is much less tolerant about problems closer to home:

> One of our drivers on his way home stopped to sleep just outside Ramsgate. When he was travelling north the next day on the motorway people were flashing their headlights at him. When he stopped he found the rear doors of the van swinging open; £3,000 worth of tools had been stolen from the vehicle while he was asleep at Ramsgate. That's good, loving, British neighbours! So you can't really get too angry about the beggars in Albania.

The response to the people when aid was given to them was deeply moving, especially in such cases as a mother being given medicines desperately needed for a sick child. There was a dignity which impressed the teams; though grateful, the recipients were not gushing in their thanks. But the underlying despair was very evident too. At times, Blythswood workers felt they were simply throwing aid into a bottomless pit, the needs were so great. When goods were distributed, there was not the same shoving and grasping as they had seen in Romania; here the people stood in groups, quietly waiting, hoping - but not expecting - that they would receive something from the van; subdued under the watchful eyes and loaded guns of the police.

The first visits were made straightforward by the help of the authorities, but Blythswood convoys were not always so fortunate. In February 1992, Philip Ross and a team attempted to enter the country from Yugoslavia with a load of hospital beds and clothes, and were met by a chief policeman whom they had dealt with on an earlier trip, when he had obliquely suggested that an unofficial cash payment to him might speed things along; when Philip ignored the hint he had let the matter drop. This time he was aggressive and commanding.

'Passports.' He almost barked the order; his eyes gleamed with self-importance. Philip handed over the team's passports. The officer's uniform was a mass of red stars.

'Visa papers.'

'In the passports.' Philip pointed to the forms.

He nodded impressively and turned the pages of the passports with a grimy finger. He was in charge of visas. It was a very important job, to judge by his behaviour. The customs officer had cleared the convoy for entry to Albania, but now the visas had to be dealt with; a much more important matter. He closed the passports and strutted into his office.

After two hours Philip Ross went looking for the visas. The policeman reappeared, looking distinctly annoyed. 'You have to wait,' he said tersely. Then he looked hard at Philip. 'Sometimes it is not necessary to wait. We'll see.'

The team sat for another hour. Through the office window they could see the policeman. He was sitting at a desk, reading a newspaper. Occasionally he puffed on a ragged cigarette. When it was reduced to a stub he ground it carefully into an ashtray.

'Last time, he wanted money,' Philip said to his colleagues. 'That's what this performance is about.'

The police chief strolled out. 'Passports soon,' he called across to the team.

'How soon?'

'Not so long. Maybe.' The hint was unmistakable.

'How long d'you think it's going to take?' asked a worried team member. 'I've got to be back in Scotland in four days.'

Philip went into the office. 'We must have our visas. We have waited three hours.'

'Not possible,' said the policeman.

'You stamped our passports last month. There is no reason why you cannot do it again. If we do not have our visas within half an hour, we shall leave. We have trucks full of supplies that the hospital in Tirana has requested. It is the Albanian law that you give us our visas.'

'The Albanian law,' relied the officer smugly, 'has changed. Now we have to telephone Tirana.'

The customs officer broke in. 'No, it is not possible to telephone. Telephone is broken.'

After half an hour's further waiting they went back into the office. The policeman and the customs officer were arguing hysterically with each other in Albanian. After watching for a quarter of an hour Philip interrupted. 'We must have our visas.'

'No visas,' snapped the policeman.

'Then we must go back,' said Philip. 'Our passports, please.'

A few minutes later, amid cloud of dust, the two officials watched an entire convoy of relief goods disappearing into the distance.[2]

In Romania, even before the Revolution, the guards had been

---

2. The end of this story is remarkable. The team took the beds all the way back to Romania and asked the Baptists in Romania what they should do. They were guided to a large cancer hospital in the city, where the director received the beds with some emotion. 'This city is the main entrance point from the West,' he said. 'Of all the relief convoys passing through, we haven't received a thing.' The clothes that the truck had been carrying were given to the families of Romanian gypsies. The incident demonstrates vividly that even in 1992, though aid was pouring into Eastern Europe in enormous quantities, there were still many pockets of need that had not been touched, and these often appeared in very unexpected places.

officious and correct, giving the appearance of following a set procedure even though that procedure sometimes seemed arbitrary and vindictive. In Albania, however, the border control officers were openly corrupt. Where at other borders a threat to go back home with the load would have worked wonders, in Albania it had no effect.

The decision made by Philip was in accordance with Blythswood policy. One bribe given - apart from any moral considerations - would have set such a precedence that Blythswood would be committed to heavy border expenditure for the indefinite future. The only exception that the Society makes, on principle, is requests for medicine that appear genuine; border guards are as entitled to help as anybody else. In this instance, Philip calculated that a big fuss at the border and the spectacle of the trucks turning round to take their relief goods elsewhere would make a point which could be further strengthened by making an even bigger protest to the Albanian authorities. In fact he found his case supported by the Albanian Encouragement Project, an aid organisation with which Blythswood was working closely at the time and which requested details of the circumstances in which aid destined for Albania had been sent away at the border.

Through the Encouragement Project's contacts, Philip's protest was made to the highest authorities. But even Philip was somewhat taken aback to receive a letter in due course from the President of Albania, apologising for the incident, promising full rights of entry in the future, and refunding the cost of visas so far purchased and adding the information that visas were shortly to be discarded for citizens of EEC member countries.

Philip was acquiring a reputation for tough negotiation with officials. He had been making monthly trips throughout the past twelve months for Blythswood, and was now a full-time member of the staff. When he had left school at seventeen, though he was qualified for university entrance he decided he would prefer to start his own business as an office supplier. He acquired something of a reputation as a local wonder (his sister Lois followed in his footsteps when in 1992 she and seven other pupils at Plockton High School won the Highland Area heat of the Young Enterprise competition: they had founded a flourishing company producing headed notepaper, and Lois was its managing director).

He continued in business for two years but developed a keen interest in all aspects of Blythswood work. He was moved by the plight of the Romanians and when he visited Romania himself his priorities changed dramatically. He gave up his business interests and worked for a period as a volunteer. During 1992 he was given the title of Overseas Projects Officer, and was put in charge of the overseas aid distribution programme. He also undertook the computerisation of Blythswood. In Jackie's opinion, 'He was the right man in the right place at the right time.' At the time of writing, Philip has begun studying for a BA at the Evangelical Theological College of Wales, but still does some work for Blythswood, with the help of a telephone computer link to the system in Lochcarron.

Unlike the Romanians, the Albanians did not always show any interest in English publications. In Romania, a book van being used by the Society for transport still had the sign on its side, 'Lochcarron Christian Books'. When it stopped it was surrounded by people wanting to buy books. Often the demand for reading matter was greater than that for food and clothes - an experience which other organisations, such as Operation Mobilisation, have also recorded. It was experiences like that which made Jackie reflect that in the future there was a great potential for Christian bookshops in Romania. But in Albania, it was often a very different situation; Jackie, asked how many times he had been asked for books, could not remember a single occasion. Philip's experience, however, was quite different. He found Albanians desperate to learn English and appreciative of any English literature they could get. On one occasion he met an Albanian customs officer who could recite John 3 in Authorised Version English.

Although a great number of Romanian requests came from people without any Christian background, the religious history of the country undoubtedly contributed to the interest in Christian literature. In Albania, by contrast, there are very few Christians, and certainly no large churches like the Second Baptist Church in Oradea. So there was no possibility of working with a church-based relief programme.

However, Jackie was put in touch with a Dutch Christian, Gesena Blauw, who lives in Albania and works for the Dutch sponsored Albanian Encouragement Project in Tirana. A woman of apparently superhuman energy, she lives in the same conditions as the Albanian people and with the support of her Dutch sponsors works closely with the Albanian government, the hospitals and the villages. There is a clear method of distribution, by which contracts are entered into with the organisations receiving aid. Blythswood is very happy to be associated with such a scheme, for it guarantees a very high degree of certainty that goods are given to the people who need them.

The complaints made by the Albanian Encouragement Project, and the President's intervention, brought about a change of personnel at the border and access for the trucks was made much easier. The problems experienced in February ceased to exist, and the convoys were able to proceed with only the relatively minor inconvenience of children throwing rocks at the vehicles because they would not stop to buy candles from roadside stalls.

Blythswood did not use the Greek route to Albania for very long; the overland route was cheaper and the paperwork much less complicated than the sea crossing from Italy. Entering Albania from the east is a dramatic but tedious business: the road winds up a hill towards a police hut and a house on either side of the gate, and a fence stretches away on either side, symbolising the isolation in which the country was kept for so long; whether the fence actually achieves anything, or what would happen if a vehicle trundled across it instead of waiting in the queue, no Blythswood driver has ever tried to find out.

During the long wait - which can sometimes be as long as five hours - a driver has time to examine the landscape many times. It is impossible not to notice the pill-box gun emplacements on the hills, some with gun barrels protruding. There is time, too, to examine the Albanian vehicles, conspicuous among the Western ones. David Fraser, who has driven Blythswood vehicles to Albania several times, likens Albanian traffic to a mobile motor museum, with ancient vehicles still in use and, in the capital, a rare Western vehicle standing out among the rest. While waiting at the border, too, one cannot fail to see the Albanians who loiter at the gate. Driver Donald MacPhail, writing after the first Blythswood trip to Albania, described: 'The gaunt look on the faces of men, women and children holding their border gates and wire, desperate to get out of their poverty. The little boys' faces with their large eyes and drawn skin shouting to us, 'Give me, give me, give me,' and pointing to their mouths.'

By mid-1992, Blythswood was working closely with the Albanian Encouragement Project. People in Scotland and further afield were contributing generously to the work. The country that had been closed was open; people who had suffered both spiritual and physical hardship were being helped. The authorities were co-operating and drivers were beginning to adapt to driving past mobs of angry children throwing stones and avoiding likely ambush places and parking sites vulnerable to pilferers. What drove them on was the need, evident on every face. Donald MacPhail reflects:

> As we experience wintry weather here let us spare a thought for our friends in Eastern Europe ... My thoughts are with those people as the temperature drops. The Children's Hospital where there are no heaters and where the water is heated on a primus stove. How necessary it is for us to establish sound contacts which can be used to distribute the food, clothing, medical supplies and

> Bibles. The lady doctor at the hospital stated, 'We have nothing. We need everything.'

Many tons of aid were taken to the Albanian hospitals, orphanages and communities. There is no doubt that lives were transformed and sometimes saved by what Blythswood was able to bring - as much in the spiritual as the physical dimension, for though no large-scale church-based relief project existed when Blythswood first went into Albania, there were Christians in the country who had remained faithful during the long years of communism. Several contacts were made, to whom Christian literature could be given for distribution. One of the most encouraging aspects of the work in Albania was the opportunity to go into schools, where Blythswood distributed copies of a book on basic biblical teachings, *Ultimate Questions*[3], and also quantities of Bibles and biblical literature, all with the permission of the authorities.

Yet Albania was not the only need. On its very doorstep a battle was now raging that threatened not only the security of the region but that of the whole continent. Through that war zone, Blythswood brought its trucks to Albania. But by the time that refugees had begun pouring out of Yugoslavia and the wholesale destruction of towns and villages had become commonplace spectacles on Western news bulletins, Blythswood was already bringing help.

---

3. John Blanchard, *Ultimate Questions* (Evangelical Press, 1987). This is a beautifully-illustrated 32-page book in full colour which presents in simple language the Bible's answers to a range of crucial issues concerning God, humanity and the problem of evil.

# 13
# The Cauldron Spills Over

> The Czechoslovak and Yugoslav principles, which had been put forward as expressions of nationalism, turned out to be ... devices for holding together peoples of different nationalities. (A.J.P. Taylor, *The Habsburg Monarchy 1809-1918*, 1948)

The two soldiers appeared in the Bosnian village out of nowhere; the only warning that they had arrived was the noise of their guns. They were shooting their automatic rifles into the air. They looked like bandits in a TV Western film, ammunition belts looped across their chests, over their shoulders, round their waists - about two hundred rounds. They were very drunk, almost out of their minds with alcohol.

The villagers had disappeared at the first sound of gunfire, but when they realised that only two men were involved they began to come back, emerging from the shells of houses that had been mortared into rubble. Some of them were living in the remnants of what had been their homes, boarding up shattered windows and patching the gaping roof somehow. The soldiers were cheering and laughing, roaring out greetings to anybody they saw, still punctur-ing the sky with shots. The villagers muttered greetings in return, mindful of the power of the weapons and fearful that the men might turn against them.

Jackie Ross watched with a strange, detached calmness. A drunk with a gun, he reflected, is a dangerous man. But he felt no fear at that time; he was used to the delayed reaction, the realisation after the event that he had been in considerable danger. But for the present he just felt a deep sadness and a rueful irony.

In the summer of 1992 the world watched, apparently impotent, as Serbs, Croats and Moslems were locked in bitter conflict in what was by then rarely called Yugoslavia any more. City after city was attacked, pounded, and systematically razed as the armies moved on: Dubrovnik, Vukovar, and then Sarajevo itself, a name already notorious in the history of twentieth-century warfare. In Britain, many of the media were noticeably pro-Croat. The scenario presented to the British people was simple and persuasive. The Serbs, it was pointed out, were engaged in a war of territorial acquisition. Serbian slogans such as 'Greater Serbia' and 'ethnic cleansing' were much quoted. The television showed pictures of appalling suffering, of long queues of refugees pouring out of the doomed cities, and it was explained that the figures involved - around three million by the end of the summer - made this the largest refugee problem since the Second World War. Some commentators drew parallels with Hitler's Final Solution, and others pointed out the obvious fact that Serbia (like her enemies) was trying to seize and hold as much territory as possible against the time the United Nations might demand a permanent cease-fire and insist that all parties in the conflict remain within the borders then existing.

Serbian aggression was undeniable, and the many examples that the media pointed out were valid ones. What was, generally speaking, conspicuously lacking from the British press coverage was an adequate historical context. Few tabloids pointed out that the bitter hatred between Serbs and Croats had its immediate origins in the period of the Second World War, when the Croatian Ustase fascist regime had embarked on a campaign masterminded by the Catholic churches who regarded the Orthodox Serbs as schismatics. The terse Ustase policy: 'Convert a third. Expel a third. Kill a third'[1] resulted in mass expulsion and massacre of Serbs.

1. Of this notorious period, Jacques Rupnik (*The Other Europe*, 1988) writes: 'In Yugoslavia the civil war caused more deaths than the brutality of German repression. This includes the nationalist ('tribal') warfare of the Croatian Ustashas against the Serbs; it also includes Communist partisans and Serbian

In 1992 the memory rankled as keenly as if the atrocities had happened only yesterday. Catholic churches in Croatia were demolished as direct revenge for incidents that had happened almost half a century previously. And yet the situation was more complex still. Many Croats argued in 1992 that had the Serbian government of the time pursued different policies towards Croats the Ustase regime would never have gained power. And yet, again, it could be argued that to assess the conflict properly one has to go even further back, to the First World War, to the Balkan Wars that immediately preceded it, and probably even further back than that.

This tinderbox of bitter resentment exploded in September 1991, after months of skirmishing following Croatia's declaration of independence on June 25. The result was the first European war since 1945. The Yugoslav Federal Forces, heavily Serb-dominated, bombarded the Croatian coast and attacked the Croat-Serbian border. At the same time Federal troops were moved into Bosnia-Hercogovina. As the ethnic tensions boiled over into massive destruction and displacement, the rest of the world watched appalled as cease-fires were brokered and ignored. As the Moslem community - left largely untouched by the Ustase reign of terror - became a Serb target too, speculation increased as to the likelihood of the conflict extending to involve countries outside the peninsula.

In December, Blythswood sent three vehicles to Yugoslavia. 'There is even greater need in Yugoslavia than elsewhere in Eastern Europe,' Jackie reported. 'That is the opinion of the drivers now returning, and they had already witnessed shocking poverty in

---

Chetnicks against the Ustashas and against each other.' Bernard Newman, in his appreciative *Tito's Yugoslavia* (1951) deplored Ustashe atrocities but argued, 'I knew that the Ustashi were not typical of the Croat people, but only examples of the degradation which can be achieved by leaders who have but one viewpoint ...' The figures achieved under the Ustase programme (which might fairly be termed 'ethnic cleansing') were: 350,000 Orthodox killed, 250,000 forcibly converted, 300,000 deported to Serbia (cf. Janice Broun, *Conscience and Captivity in Eastern Europe* 1988, p.249) .

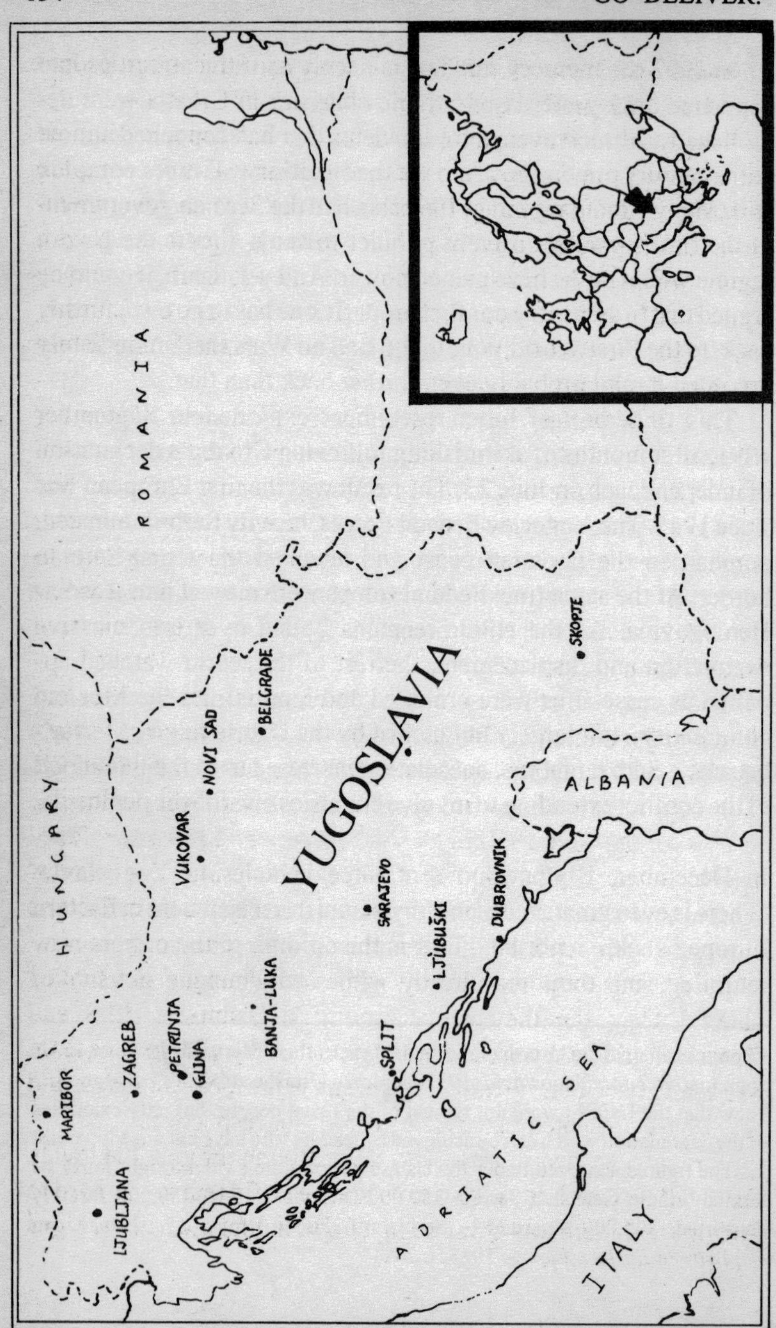
HUNGARY
ROMANIA
YUGOSLAVIA
ALBANIA
ITALY
ADRIATIC SEA
LJUBLJANA
MARIBOR
ZAGREB
PETRINJA
GLINA
BANJA-LUKA
VUKOVAR
NOVI SAD
BELGRADE
SARAJEVO
LJUBUŠKI
SPLIT
DUBROVNIK
SKOPJE

Romania and Albania. In Yugoslavia they have seen people homeless, without food, and without a change of clothing.'

Two articulated lorries and a seven-and-a-half ton truck entered Yugoslavia from Szeged in southern Hungary. The lorries were carrying food and clothing; the smaller truck was carrying medicine. On the way in, drivers of other convoys they met up with bound for other destinations were astonished to hear where they were going. 'You're mad - they'll attack you, they're already shooting at Red Cross convoys. You'll be ambushed. You'll lose the lorries at least.'

By the time they reached the border they were wondering whether they should go on, but the fighting was very localised and they were travelling in a part of the country from which the war had already moved on. After consulting Red Cross representatives they decided to go on. There was a good deal of laughter and jokes to keep each other's spirits up, but each of the drivers confessed later that when alone with his thoughts in the cab, there had been butterflies in his stomach.

Their route took them to Novi-Sad (where, ironically, there had been a major church conference a few years earlier on the subject of ethnic reconciliation), and down to Banja Luka in the foothills of the mountains. They were travelling along the river, following the line of the Croatian border, and there was constant military activity - many road checks, tanks manoeuvring, and several bridges that had been blown up and temporary structures erected alongside, protected by gun emplacements. The soldiers who stopped them at the road checks were very young, some looked about fifteen; but they were carrying Kalashnikov rifles and ammunition. There were checks at almost every village. The team had been given identification documents in the local language, and these were presented innumerable times for inspection.

For most of their journey they were driving through the lovely Sava valley, which looked so calm and peaceful that it was hard to imagine that there was a war being fought not far away. Few signs of damage to buildings could be seen.

At Banja Luka the lorries came to a halt and the drivers got out, looking round at a town that seemed to be very affected by the fighting that was going on nearby, though there were soldiers everywhere. The only obvious sign that war had touched Banja Luka was the little white plaques that were fixed to the walls of many houses. They had black surrounds and a name inscribed. It was the local sign of a house mourning the dead.

In the bitter cold their breath made white curls of steam in the air as they talked. David Fraser, one of the drivers, had the telephone number of their contacts: Milan and Brenda Tovarloza, whom the Rosses had first visited in 1988. Milan was now pastor of a church in Banja Luka. David dialled the number with fingers so cold they could hardly feel the dial. It seemed an age before Milan appeared in his car and led them to his apartment.

They were shown into a warm room, where the feeling began to come back into their arms and legs as they drank tea and ate supper. After talking for a while the team decided to go to bed. Their room turned out to be unheated and was so cold that they would have been warmer if they had slept in the vans. Two of the team were unable to sleep and lay in the darkness, listening to the thumping of shells exploding in the distance and watching the flashes of gunfire on the horizon. The war sounded a long way off, but its effects were plain to see in Banja Luka, where their hosts had only enough fuel to heat one room.

The next day they delivered their goods to a Red Cross depot in the town, a large building full of bags of flour and other foodstuffs and goods of all kinds. The refugee camps themselves were inaccessible; nobody was allowed near them and they were protected by armed guards.

David Fraser made two further trips to Yugoslavia in January, then did not go again until September 1992, when he drove one of two vehicles, the other being driven by Graham MacSween, now almost recovered from his injuries and still committed to helping Eastern Europe. They entered through Slovenia, a region that had declared independence at the same time as Croatia. Slovenia's war had been short and decisive. Always a place where the Yugoslavian rich lived, it was still prosperous, relatively undamaged by fighting. Their first destination was the town of Maribor, just across the border from Austria. Maribor was a wealthy town, many of whose residents owned holiday villas on the Adriatic coast; David and Graham looked in awe at shops that reached Parisian standards of luxury. At the Red Cross depot in Maribor, refugees helped them unload. A translator was assigned to them, a talkative woman who answered all their questions. 'It is as if there has never been a war here,' she said. 'People live their lives just the same as before.'

David left his lorry in Maribor and joined Graham for the next part of the journey, towards Split on the Dalmatian coast. They were advised to take a ferry from Rijeka, which meant following the course of the northern border of the old Yugoslavia. They drove past Ljubljana and found that they were following what was now the border between Slovenia and Croatia. The television pundits' talk of 'redrawing the borders' here took physical form. Everything was new; what had been a through road was now a border post, with spacious parking areas, newly constructed offices and administrative buildings.

At the ferry the lorry was persuaded into the ship by some clever manoeuvring - there was an inch clearance - and some diplomatic bargaining with the captain, who was very unwilling to take the vehicle. In the end, for a fare of £260, the truck was allowed to stay and Graham and David enjoyed a twelve-hour Adriatic cruise down to Split. In the seventy-or-so mile journey on inland, the truck was stopped at several check points and crossed another new border.

They unloaded at the fire station in a small town where there had been recent fighting, and afterwards were taken around the town to see the war damage. Several houses were barricaded with sandbags, others had shattered windows; occasionally they would see a roofless house, its interior burnt out. Many buildings were pocked with bullet holes, trees had branches blasted off, the bank had suffered a direct hit.

'You read about this in your British newspapers,' said their guide. They were standing in a street still littered with rubble. 'A mortar landed here. Two children were killed by shrapnel. They even kill children. But why not? They tried to shell the hospital, but they kept missing. They will kill anybody they can.'

His companions knew that for every Serb atrocity, they had been told by the other side of Croat atrocities; but what made it peculiarly horrifying was that both sides would sometimes be telling a story of some savage act, and the team would only gradually realise that it had happened half a century ago.

The first contacts Blythswood had with the Yugoslavian people were with the Serbian community, through Milan and Brenda: a number of loads were delivered to Banja Luka, where they were distributed among local, Serbian people; then at Milan's suggestion they delivered to the Red Cross. The aid they gave through the Red Cross to refugees was distributed among Serbs and Croats coming out of Croatia. But though the first contact was with Serbs that does not imply an endorsement of the Serbian cause, any more than the aid given to Croatian refugees constitutes an endorsement of theirs.

In much of Yugoslavia there were no people to help any more. Vukovar, the site of a long and tenacious defence against overwhelming odds, was virtually reduced to rubble; Philip Ross reported that he did not see any undamaged buildings. Walls were knocked down, roofs demolished, shells fired into the interiors - it seemed a deliberate and methodical attempt to make the whole city uninhabitable. Military observers have deduced that the later Serbian bombardment of Sarajevo was an attempt to obliterate the city as a focus of Croatian identity. Such attacks were part of an overall strategy: to blast a Serbian corridor through Croatian territory to link two areas of predominantly Serb population. This, the

Serbians argued, would protect them against any persecution ... After all, history showed that persecution by the Croats was very likely.

But tragically, what history shows is that revenge breeds revenge. Blythswood watched helplessly as whole communities were displaced and reports of massacres were broadcast on the news. It was to settle old scores: but it was creating new scores that would need to be settled in their turn. In this apparently irrevocable cycle of destruction and killing, while world leaders negotiated cease-fire after cease-fire and watched them all fail, and first one and then another party walked out of peace conference after peace conference, Blythswood and other relief agencies continued to bring in food, Bibles, clothes, Christian literature and medicine.

Philip Ross made monthly visits to Eastern Europe and wrote full reports on his return. They are documents written with the matter-of-fact stark clarity of the eyewitness; the fact that they were written at all is an indication that Blythswood was there, offering practical and spiritual help. The following is Philip's report from the Spring 1992 newsletter.

The towns of Petrinja and Glina in the Serbian enclave of Kraijina in Croatia were our destination. Petrinja was once a bustling town of 20,000 people. Petrinja now has only a few shell shocked inhabitants and masses of army personnel. The remaining inhabitants have a strange, wide-eyed look. They all want tranquillisers. Most of them use slivovitz plum brandy as their tranquilliser. Houses stand on the street, windows and doors left wide open. Look in and you see beds with the covers thrown back and wardrobes half empty. Something must have caused great alarm. People have left in a great hurry. Perhaps they escaped to safety. Perhaps they met their final destination in the next street.

Glina is different. It's not on the front line any more. Life has returned to semi-normality. In Glina we delivered food and medicine to the hospital, where many of the war wounded still lay in bed. The Catholic church lay ruined. The Serbs had destroyed it because the Croats had killed 1,500 Serbs in the Orthodox church during World War II. A church for a church. They claimed the blood had been ankle deep.

In Glina we met Dr Bani. Dr Bani had come from Belgrade to work as a volunteer. Dr Bani was angry. He was angry because all the soldiers were drunk. He was angry because the Croats gave the journalists nice hotels in Zagreb and told them all about the Serbian atrocities. He was angry because the Serbs gave them parking tickets in Belgrade and never told about any of the Croatian atrocities. Dr Bani's friends from the TV station wanted to show us a film they had made during the war, of Serbs that had been killed by Croats. The film showed men who had rocket launchers fired at their heads, women who had had the skin cut around their waists and pulled over their heads and one man whose feet had been chopped off with an axe. In his last desperate moments, as his life was swallowed up in the darkness of death, he had tied ropes round his legs to try to stop the bleeding. Probably he died without any real hope. Too bad. Too bad nobody heard the call to 'Go into all the world, and preach the gospel' to that man. Too bad for that man the only hope he had was the priest chanting at his funeral. We saw that on the video too.

That night we drove through villages where these people had died. We drove past their houses, now ruined, burnt and empty. People in Glina were afraid of Croat hit and run squads coming out of the forest at night. We were too. It's hard to recognise British number plates in the dark. Peasants stand alongside the road, armed with rifles and machine guns. They flash their torches trying to stop passing vehicles. The war has made them a little crazy. One man demanded to know where we had been when the fighting was going on. He said, 'I'm the boss here now.' It was a relief to get out of Kraijina, out of Yugoslavia. It wouldn't have taken long for us to become like the paranoid people of Petrinja.

What does the future hold for those people? What, indeed, should the future role of Blythswood be in this situation?

At the time of writing, nobody knows. It may be a long, drawn-out war, or it may be over very suddenly. In a very real sense that is not Blythswood's concern. The task is to help those in need, whether it be with bandages, food, Bibles or clothing. Any longer-term programme is the business of politicians.

# 14
# Blythswood Today

> By the end of Spring, [Blythswood's] mercy fleet, which now includes four 38-ton articulated lorries, will have made close on 100 runs from its depot on Strathpeffer Road ... carrying hundreds of tons not only of food, clothing and medical supplies, but also of anything from paper and pens to pick-axes and ploughs; safety-pins to cement mixers; toys and tin-openers to tattie-seeders or tractors ... and, of course, Christian literature and Bibles. (*Executive*, May/June 1992)

It would be a neat and satisfying way to end this book if it were possible to announce the completion of Blythswood's programme. But it is a story without an end, at least so far as any human eye can see. Each day's newspapers tell of more suffering, of renewed crises in areas where it had been thought peace had been restored and of new catastrophes often undreamed of and unplanned for. Blythswood exists to help those in physical and spiritual need, and will go on doing so. Today's Albania is tomorrow's Somalia, but tomorrow Albania will still be suffering; so will Somalia; so will countless others. The question is not when Blythswood will consider its task complete, but on what project will it spend its finite resources next. It is an attitude that recalls Mother Teresa's comment, made in the gutters and hovels of Calcutta: 'When there are no more poor, no more hungry, no more lepers - then we will retire to our convent and give ourselves entirely to prayer. But I hardly think that time will come ...'

To refer twice to a prominent Roman Catholic in a book about a mission of a Scottish Presbyterian Church may raise some eyebrows. But it is entirely characteristic of Blythswood, who help people of all faiths and none. To those who do not know the work well there is sometimes a perplexity at the juxtaposition of a theologically 'narrow' view of church life and the creation of one of the most effective mobile relief task forces among all independent aid organisations. Some Christians argue that the priority ought to be to bring people into the church and teach them from the pulpit; some who are not Christians cannot understand why Blythswood hampers (in their view) its aid programme by adhering to old-fashioned and unworldly prejudices. The following letter from a newspaper, after an incident that received some publicity in summer 1992, reflects this:

> I am referring to the front-page story *Charity refuses Lairg show's cheque* (July 31) - the charity being the Blythswood Trust. According to the story, the Rev. Jackie Ross said that a Christian organisation could not condone fund-raising by way of dances or licensed events. Well, Mr Ross, would you like to alienate even more people from Christianity by presenting it as being stuffy, irrelevant and belonging to some dark age? (*Northern Times*, 7 August 1982)

Making due allowance for the fact that newspaper controversy rarely presents the case of accuser or accused in the best light, and for the inevitable misunderstandings that arise from second-hand reporting, this was an unfortunate mistake in the eyes of many; though the following extract from the Society's *Guidelines For Blythswood Workers Abroad* shows that the Society's attitude to alcohol reflects some very practical considerations:

> 4. Alcohol and smoking can be offensive to some Christians in some countries: please be sensitive. Drunkenness and drink-driving are inexcusable.

In any case, Blythswood's critics are being unrealistic. The Society is not an anonymous organisation composed of people from such varying backgrounds that it has no corporate identity. It is a project of a minor non-conformist denomination, and it is not surprising that it reflects the way of life of the people from whom it grew. Such a way of life may not be to everybody's taste, but it is not possible to separate the two. For the same reason, those who criticise the Society's adherence to the Authorised Version of the Bible in preference to versions in modern speech, its use of literature that on the whole refrains from any attempt to be 'contemporary' for its own sake, and its insistence on maintaining a literature distribution work that attracts far less funding than the relief programme and uses space in the office that might be used for relief workers, have misunderstood not only who Blythswood are, but the reason for the results it has achieved.[1] No apologies are needed.

But even that is to mistake the central point. Rather nearer the mark is the fact that Blythswood is not a relief organisation that happens to be led by Christians. It is a Christian organisation that happens to be a relief organisation. Nor is it just a matter of Christians looking for some worthy cause to adopt. These Christians are driven by the essential teaching of their faith. Blythswood literature is punctuated by references to Bible passages that place upon Christians a responsibility to help those who are in need, to feed not only their own people but all who are hungry and in despair. One of the most moving moments in the 1992 Blythswood video *Bringing Good News from a Far Country* comes right at the beginning, before any of the shattering images of need that follow. It is the reading (in the Authorised Version) of this passage:

---

1. Though, it is worth pointing out, the majority of literature sent out by the Society is sent at the request of individuals who have specifically applied for it; and the chief recipients of the literature - Africans, and particularly Nigerians and Ghanaians - have a decided preference for the Authorised Version and for the writing style adopted by the authors the Blythswood distributes. *Let's Study Mark and Acts,* for example, has been used by thousands of students in Africa, but the Society has received no suggestions from the Africans that a more modern version and approach might be more effective.

> And when ye reap the harvest of your land, thou shalt not wholly reap the corners of thy field, neither shalt thou gather the gleanings of thy harvest ... Thou shalt leave them for the poor and stranger; I am the LORD your God (Leviticus 19:9-10).

The Bible affirms that compassion is not merely an option.

Is that then the core of the Blythswood ethos? Not quite. Those who have been involved in the work would rarely explain their motivation in terms of 'duty' or quote Bible verses like the one above. One Blythswood worker, a Scot, Bill Ritchie who drove in a convoy to Serbia, returned with this comment:

> We're sitting here in this lovely country of Scotland, and out there people are so destitute, so butchered, it's just not true ... And yet the people are so nice, so co-operative and so helpful. And when they discovered that we were Christians, that touched them. For they have been brought up for the past three or four decades under an atheistic philosophy. And to think that Christians out here could think about them ... Oh, my, it was worth it, just to see their faces ...

Compassion, for Blythswood, is not a chore but an outflowing. It is a logical consequence of being a Christian; it is not what a Christian does but what a Christian is. And in putting compassion into practice they are joined by supporters of all faiths and none. People are important. It's important to have the right people to help, people who can encourage and motivate individuals, churches, companies and charities to help. Jackie Ross describes it as follows:

> It would never work without the volunteers - from the people who come in through the Manse door and help to sort out a bag of clothes, discarding what isn't very good, to the people who drive the vehicles. What amazes me is that people seem to be out there wanting to do something, and we seem to be a meeting point, a point of contact for them whereby they can do what they feel they should be doing ... and that's good.

Bill Shannon, scriptwriter of the Blythswood video, sums it up:

> Lots of people doing what they should be doing. Doing what their Christian conscience tells them they should be doing. And doing it for their fellow man, in the name of God.

To complete this survey of the Blythswood story, a few highlights from 1992.

The appointment of Donald Macleod marked a major step forward for the Blythswood. A native of Stornoway, he had lived in New Zealand where his father was a minister, and came back to England to work for the Council for the Abuse of Alcohol. When Jackie Ross approached him he was back in Scotland, living in Dingwall, where he became a volunteer helper at Blythswood's depot. Jackie was impressed by Donald's willingness to get his hands dirty, the understanding he showed of the needs of Eastern Europe and the issues Blythswood was facing in a changing world, his experience with a caring organisation and his ability to communicate. He also warmed to Donald's deep personal faith, which he shared with his parents who were both outstanding Christians.

Jackie offered Donald a full-time post with Blythswood. He accepted, and became Blythswood's first Appeals Co-ordinator.

Up to that point, the Society's publicity had consisted of advertising taken out in newspapers under the guidance of an advertising space salesman. Donald brought a new perspective. He understood the world of public relations, and his work with the Alcohol Abuse Council had given him a wealth of experience and know-how. At Blythswood, he introduced a pattern of targeted advertising, carefully selecting the best places to advertise and producing advertisements tailored to the context they were to be published in.

Donald was full of ideas for bringing Blythswood to the notice of the public and potential sponsors. It quickly became clear that he would need secretarial help, and an advertisement was placed in the local press. There was a large response. Among those who applied were many married women.

After appointing Donald's secretary, Jackie Ross reflected on the interest that the advertisement had produced. Here were a large number of married women, often with grown-up families, and with a great desire to be involved in the Blythswood's activities. Perhaps there was a way that they too could be involved. So the idea was born of the Blythswood charity shops, staffed by many of the women who had answered the advertisement. He noted the idea in a memo:

> Would it be possible to set up some shops? Having done some research it does seem possible that such shops would not be a burden on the Society. They would have the added advantage of:
>
> 1. Raising public awareness of Blythswood's work.
> 2. Acting in a small way as an outlet for Christian literature.
> 3. Providing inexpensive clothes for some in real need.
> 4. Very usefully, acting as aid collection points.
> 5. An avenue for usefulness for Christians who wish to help.
> 6. Most importantly, raising funds for our work from a number who could not support in any other way than by buying what is useful for themselves.

At the time this book goes to press, the idea is being actively considered by the Blythswood leadership.

At Lochcarron James MacDonald, who has been in charge of the Scripture distribution programme for the past seven years, reports that the work has in no way been overtaken by the more publicised work of the Society in Eastern Europe. 'We are glad to report that in the first two months of this year we were able to post 11,375 copies of *Let's Study Mark and Acts*.' - in the first quarter of 1990, 4,245 copies had been despatched.

> About 500 completed papers were received in the same two months, qualifying for the free Bible. At the time of writing we have 1,500 copies packed and awaiting postage and another 2,000

> labels typed. With our stock of *Let's Study Mark and Acts* down to under 5,000 copies the prospect of a reprint looms on the horizon - something which requires a lot of capital. Almost nine years have passed since we embarked on this method of Scripture distribution and we are grateful to all whose support has enabled it to continue, not least to the voluntary markers who provide a personal response to each student.

James was also able to report distribution of French tracts throughout French-speaking Africa, and free tracts to evangelists working among West African prisoners.

By the early summer, Blythswood's vehicles were active all over Eastern Europe. One month's schedule is typical. Four vehicles left Ramsgate on 31 May. Two went through Romania to Belgrade; on arrival there on 6 June, one went on to Albania. A third completed a round trip to Cluj and Oradea in Romania in ten days and immediately set out again for Kiev in the Ukraine. The fourth vehicle was going to Romania.

The day after the four vehicles left, a fifth left Glasgow heading for Romania; it would make two round trips there in the same month. A sixth vehicle left Stornoway two days later bound for Albania, and for the whole of this period Philip Ross was driving a seventh vehicle on an itinerary that included Oradea, Belgrade, Kiev and Bucharest.

Of the trips made that summer, the following brief extracts from drivers' reports can serve as examples.

> [Romania] Our hosts are a Christian couple with a family of eight. Under cover of darkness we take parcels of clothes etc. to selected homes. Some are no more than shacks, yet some of the Lord's dear people live here. What joy on their faces as they receive gifts! ... Around midnight we knocked at another door. A man in his 40s lives here with his wife and two children. It was afterwards we learned that he had come home drunk and battered his wife who was a believer. How must he have felt when complete strangers with gifts of clothing etc. stood in his doorstep that very night?

[Albania] As we passed through villages we noticed in one what passed for a hospital. I would have called it a shack ... We subsequently visited a hospital on the outskirts of Tirana where we delivered a refrigerator - they had none. Here I had to walk on pallets of wood to get over puddles in the corridor. These corridors were devoid of all lighting - and this was a hospital for malnourished children.

[Yugoslavia] After being held up at the German-Austrian border, along with a UN convoy, one of our two trucks destined for Yugoslavia eventually arrived. Our load was to be distributed among refugees in Belgrade. Many refugees from the Croatian and Bosnian war zones are living in temporary accommodation, hotels and in the open air. They are easily spotted in Belgrade, dressed as country people and carrying their possessions in cardboard boxes.

[Ukraine] Kiev's full of grey apartment blocks with the occasional old building. It has a big river running through it which is rather nice. As soon as we arrived the sky was lit up with a spectacular flash and suddenly the lights went out and all the trams stopped ... basically the trip consisted of driving to places, emptying the lorries and getting back.

[Iasi, Romania] Delivered an upright freezer cabinet for storing medicines to the orphanage, plus large quantities of baby milk, medicines, blankets, washing powder etc. New cots, toys, clean sheet are evidence of a big improvement in this particular orphanage. Yet all this was tinged with sadness when we were told that a number of babies were HIV positive ....

Such a programme of aid requires much more storage and administration space than is available at Dingwall. During 1992 Blythswood was hunting desperately for new accommodation; the Dingwall premises had always been temporary, and the owners had regretfully had to give Jackie notice that they would be requiring part of them again.

Knowing that there were hangars at Alness, Jackie approached several of the companies that owned them, including Christian Salvenson the hauliers. He thought that Dr Salvenson would be too busy with his business activities to be at all approachable, but when he rang him he received a very positive response: 'I'll be at Alness tomorrow - I'll meet you there.' When Jackie met him the next day and explained his problem he was immediately sympathetic and gave Jackie full use of a hangar. Jackie discovered later that Dr Salvenson too was committed to charitable work. His son had died of leukaemia, and he was setting up a trust to fund leukaemia research. He has continued to take a keen interest in Blythswood's various activities and projects.

The new premises at Alness mark the beginning of a new phase in Blythswood's story: the administration remains at Lochcarron, but it is hoped to consolidate all the transport and loading side of the work at Alness. The Dingwall premises, though reduced in size, continue in use as a collection place, storage for the more delicate goods such as medical supplies, and an office from which Donald Macleod organises his fundraising appeals.

# 15
# The Future

> Many people in both Eastern and Western Europe - more than in the United States - regard the church as a vestige of former eras when faith and superstition predominated over scientific knowledge. But to those who long to climb out of the swamp of indifference, alienation, ethical relativism, secularization, and agnosticism, the church will always be a rock that provides faith and certainty to some, shelter to those in doubt. (Janice Broun, *Conscience and Captivity*, 1988)

What then of the future?

At the time of writing, Blythswood is preparing its autumn 1992 programme of relief trips against a background of rising uncertainty in Eastern Europe. Tensions in Yugoslavia show no real sign of resolution in any long-term political sense, and the extent to which the West is prepared to become involved is still a matter of much discussion. A particularly worrying aspect of the war for Blythswood is the fact that several relief convoys, Red Cross bases and air relief flights have been fired on by the combatants. In the longer perspective, the role of Turkey and Greece, should the Serbian offensive turn towards Kosovo and Albania, has been the subject of speculation and concern, and the question of how long borders will remain open and transit rights be granted to relief convoys through intermediate countries is still an uncertain one.

Blythswood avoids long-term plans and crystal-ball gazing. In fact Jackie Ross sees the organisation itself - as opposed to the task it fulfils - as relatively unimportant.

> I think it's possible to reach a stage where you look at the figures and you see the work expanding, the income rising, the media taking more and more interest. And then when it starts to dip again you panic and think "What's happening?" I don't think that matters very much. Of course it matters that people should continue to give to the poor so long as that need exists; and the poor we have always with us ... And it matters that people should distribute God's word, because that need is always there too. So as long as there's a need there should be people doing something about it. But you can get too attached to organisations.

The danger, as the Blythswood leadership is well aware, is that of keeping the organisation going just because it is an organisation. It's a source of satisfaction that the possessions of the Society are minimal. There is no money tied up in buildings. Some money is invested in vehicles, but the vehicles are a depreciating asset and in a few years would be written off anyway. If Blythswood ceased its work tomorrow, there would not be many assets to dispose of.

Jackie Ross, as President, has little desire to be a figurehead for the sake of it. Blythswood is not a missionary society and is not even an international relief agency in the sense that Oxfam, TEAR Fund and Christian Aid are. Were it to shut down tomorrow, the only concern its leaders would have would be to ensure that the needs Blythswood is meeting were met by others and that its existing obligations were met. The death of the Society, if it happened because its role was finished, would not be much mourned.

'We don't have ambitions to erect a large headquarters block - *The Blythswood Building*,' reflects Jackie. 'In fact I'm quite proud of our second-hand wooden buildings that we bought and put up in Lochcarron. They'll last just as long as stone if we look after them properly.'

But no organisation can rest on its laurels and do things the way they have always been done. Blythswood cannot stand still, and does not intend to. One of the benefits of operating with very little baggage is that the Society is able to react to changing situations and, like a highly mobile task force, reallocate and redeploy its forces. Because it has not invested in complicated and restrictive management systems, it is also possible to constantly review the way the operation proceeds from day to day and to keep its whole financial strategy under constant review.

Donald Macleod, as Appeals Co-ordinator, has seen considerable changes since his appointment, not least in the level of giving. In a country which has been hard hit by one of the severest economic recessions since the war, the continuing flood of money and goods from the general public, industry and organisations is astonishing. Coupled with a general rise of interest in the work of Blythswood - as opposed to giving to Blythswood because it happens to be collecting for a cause which is currently receiving widespread media attention - this adds up to a trend that seems to fly in the face of generalisations about 'aid fatigue' and other easy formulations, and also in the face of hard facts such as the statistic that in 1992 national charitable giving was down by two to three percent. A simple example is the income statement for the Society for 1991 and 1992. For the whole of 1991 the total cash donations received totalled £260,000. The total for January to October 1992 is £340,000 and Blythswood income looks like reaching £400,000 for 1992.

For that reason, summer 1992 was a time to take stock and consider the way forward.

Several administrative changes were made. For example, the ownership of the vehicles was reviewed. In the early days of the Society a decision had been made with the purpose of keeping the Society's overheads and assets as low as possible: there would be no company cars or Blythswood vans. It was a good decision in the days when Blythswood was a small publishing organisation within reach of public transport and a post office; but now its activities involved transporting huge quantities of aid and literature and it owned a fleet of vehicles. As each vehicle had been acquired it had been registered in the name of John Walter Ross: somebody had to own the vehicles, and Blythswood's rules did not allow the Society to do so. Jackie neither wanted nor received any benefit from the arrangement, it involved needless paperwork and administration, and if it had been inappropriate for a Tract Society to own vehicles it was just as inappropriate for an Associated Presbyterian minister to own a fleet of lorries. The obvious decision was made - much to Jackie's satisfaction - to transfer ownership of all Blythswood vehicles to Blythswood itself.

Similar changes were made in the administrative structure to regularise methods and procedures that had grown up over the years when Blythswood was much smaller. The whole Blythswood operation was transformed when it was computerised, under the supervision of Philip Ross. Described by Jackie Ross as 'by far the biggest change that has taken place in the running of Blythswood', the task was achieved, like everything else in Blythswood, by donations of cash, equipment and time. Those who fear that Blythswood is entering a period of soulless high technology, however, should spend an evening in the Ross home, where a bewildering labyrinth of telephones in almost every room constantly interrupts meals and everyday activity. Jackie (at the time of writing) is adamantly refusing to install an answering machine.

Another area where Donald decided to invest substantial time and energy was in telling the general public how an operation like Blythswood had to run. By the middle of the summer the hangar in Alness was almost full, and goods were arriving faster than they could be taken to Eastern Europe. 200 tons of aid stayed in the hangar, and 20 tons at Dingwall, for several weeks before they began moving out again. The problem was that many people did not understand that goods, however necessary and however valuable, needed to be supported by cash. The preparation and packing of each vehicle's load, the administrative details of preparing it for its journey, the costs of the journey itself (including food and basic costs for the people travelling on the convoy), and the overhaul and maintenance of the vehicle on its return all demanded money.

Donald began a campaign to raise money as well as goods. Blythswood had always been supported by cash gifts, as the painstaking acknowledgements in the early Blythswood magazines shows. But very little of that money had gone on administration; almost all of it had gone directly into the work, whether it be the fund for Franco's support or the printing bill for the latest supply of Bibles. Now the scale of the operation is such that cash is the essential lubricant for a smooth flow of aid.

A question that is often asked is: How much does it cost to take a vehicle to Eastern Europe? This is a question that Blythswood takes care to ask itself regularly too. With a constant flow of vehicles crossing the continent, each needing paperwork, documentation, visas, fuel and other costs, the only efficient way of controlling finances is to keep watch on what proportion of the total cost of the consignment the actual costs of travel represent. A journey to deliver five hundred pounds' worth of aid at a travel cost of a thousand pounds would not be a very effective way of helping anybody.

The results of internal audit by the Society have been very encouraging. The value of second-hand goods and donated products can be difficult to estimate, but one useful guide is their value in the countries they go to. On the basis of street-market prices, calculating what, for example, a second-hand coat in good condition would fetch at market in Oradea, and adding the known value of medical and other goods whose second-hand value is easier to ascertain, it has been estimated that the cost of transport, inclusive of all outgoing and overheads, is about five percent of the total value of the consignment. For example, a black plastic bag full of clothing would be worth in Romanian terms about £25 (this information was supplied by Tom Ross, whose work with the gypsy community has already been described). The cost of getting that bag to Romania is £1 (these figures are based, of course, on the fact that each vehicle is carrying a huge number of bags). Of course the figure fluctuates; transporting seed potatoes, for example, is much more expensive than taking clothes. But on average the figure is around five percent. The figure is a very good one, but it highlights very clearly why cash has become a major priority. Each trip has its own costs, and finding the goods to take is not enough: the money has to be found, too, to take them.

Another, related, question - and a quite legitimate one, in view of the well-publicised expenditure of one or two charities on expensive facilities and high reimbursement for key staff - is the cost of general administration. Administration costs are often a matter of concern to people contemplating giving to charitable work. Many who would otherwise give generously to large charities are put off by the apparent expenses of the operation and the high percentage of their donation which they are afraid will be diverted to administration. If one donates £1,000 to the poor of Albania and £200 is used to defray office expenses in Britain, one might well think that there must be better ways of helping the poor. It is always difficult to correctly assess how much a charity spends on administration. A charity involved in giving legal aid would certainly spend more in percentage terms than would a charity helping the homeless. It is vital to consider administration costs in the light of how much work a charity does.

Blythswood's administration costs at 4 percent of all expenditure is remarkably low in any case, but astonishingly low when one takes into consideration the fact that Blythswood expects to send 2,000 tonnes of relief goods to Eastern Europe in 1992 - not to mention Scripture distribution. Blythswood's overheads are minimal, as has been said already. Full-time staff are paid reasonable salaries but hardly luxurious ones. Almost all the specialist equipment is donated free of charge, and voluntary help has been vital in the development of the work. Those who are salaried work much longer hours than they are paid for, and most are expert at several tasks far beyond their job description.

The total administrative costs of Blythswood can only be

estimated, because it is not possible to itemise accurately the amount of cross-over between the literature work and aid relief work. However, a fairly accurate estimate is possible. Approximately sixty percent of Blythswood's income goes on travel, maintenance of vehicles, and expenses incurred while travelling - for example visas, documentation, insurance and subsistence. A small percentage of the remainder is used for purchase of goods: though Blythswood actually buys very little - almost everything it takes to Eastern Europe is donated - some medical items and other specific requests are sometimes purchased out of general funds (an important point is that Blythswood's reputation, contacts, budget and expertise mean that often the money can be spent more effectively than an individual could spend the same money - for example, making use of bulk discounts and quantity buying). The rest of Blythswood's income goes on literature distribution, printing costs and other related outgoings.

Blythswood sees the stewardship of so much charitable giving as a major responsibility, and its procedures are designed to make sure that everything is done correctly and that all income and expenditure is properly accounted for. Banking is done in Lochcarron, which is the address given on Blythswood publicity and to which, therefore, most money sent by post goes. Money collected elsewhere is forwarded or credited to Lochcarron.

Receipts are issued when requested, though many donors understand that this costs money and waive acknowledgement. Where names and addresses are supplied (many gifts arrive anonymously) the donor is added to the mailing list for the Blythswood newsletter. The accounts are handled in Lochcarron, and are separate from those of the Christian bookshop with which it shares premises. The Society's accountant for many years has been Roderick Mackenzie of Tain, a member of the family that now own Christian Focus Publications. Two members of the Lochcarron staff work full-time on the accounts, which are now fully computerised.

There are, of course, statutory requirements on Blythswood to maintain good accounts, though the charity law in Scotland is different to that in England. Until 1992 the Society was not obliged to publish detailed accounts or to indicate in what ways it was seeking to fulfil its declared objectives. But from 1992 Scottish charity law changed, and it became obligatory to produce an annual report and highly detailed accounts, and to be accountable to the Secretary of State for Scotland as well as to the general public. In view of these requirements the Trustees decided to appoint as auditors Neville Russell, Chartered Accountants - a major national firm who have particular experience in dealing with the accounts of charities.

The new arrangements are designed to bring Scottish charity legislation in line with that of England and Wales, and to ensure that charities set up for a particular purpose, and benefiting from various charity exemptions, continue to pursue the objectives which were the basis for those exemptions in the first place. From Blythswood's point of view, though they involve more detailed book keeping, they do not really change anything, and in fact provide the public with better access to its accounts, an arrangement which the Society is entirely happy.

The Society's charitable status means that none of its income is paid in direct taxation. It is exempt from VAT (a much-publicised and recurring problem that Bob Geldof encountered when launching his Band Aid relief project), which saves considerable accounting costs, and being a charity means that there are distinct advantages so far as the administration of the vehicles are concerned. The costs of running the Blythswood fleet are much lower than those involved in, for example, running a haulage company.

Some who have supported Blythswood over many years have expressed a worry that it might be impossible to resist expanding into a huge impersonal organisation rapidly losing touch with the people who are its main resource. But this is unlikely to happen; in fact Blythswood intends quite the opposite.

As the work expands and the reputation of the Society grows, the vision is growing too for a much deeper mutual commitment between Blythswood and its supporters. The conventional fund-raising methods are still being used: the mobile advertising vehicles, the exhibition buses, and high-profile media events are all expertly managed by Donald MacLeod, and amply justify themselves in terms of money and goods given by people who might perhaps give once or twice, even on impulse, without forming any long-term commitment to the Society. This giving is greatly appreciated, and much of what Blythswood has been able to achieve, especially at moments of crisis such as the aftermath of the Romanian revolution and the appeal for the air ambulance fund after the tragic accident in 1991, has been financed largely by donations in collecting boxes or small anonymous gifts through the post.

But what the Society and its supporters have demonstrated is that compassion need not be a one-off, once a year event like the TV telethons and massive rock concerts that have been so much in the news. Biblically, compassion is not an occasional act at all. Against the prevailing philosophy of the West, compassion, for Blythswood, is not a matter of tossing the occasional crumb from the table of the rich but of sharing, of sacrificially giving what you have as part not of a charity bonanza but as part of your daily life.

And so Donald MacLeod as Appeals Co-ordinator has set a double target for Blythswood.

Firstly, to challenge its supporters to see the work as a long-term project, a commitment not to some abstract concept of 'relief' but to people who are our neighbours. What can we do to support them, for as long as they need support? A very effective piece of publicity that illustrates this approach was the tabloid newsletter simply describing a number of cases of need in Eastern Europe and asking repeatedly, 'Do you think this person is your friend, your neighbour? If so, will you help him?'

Secondly, to say to the churches in particular that here is an illustration of what it means to be Christ's disciples. Church membership and commitment are not just a matter of going to a particular building on Sunday once or maybe twice and taking part in a service. It is something that affects one's entire life, on weekdays as well as Sundays; and a Christian has to consider his or her responsibilities for care and compassion as part of that integrated, whole-of-life Christianity. 'Compassion isn't just an optional extra that you add on to your Christian life,' says Donald. To encourage such commitment, he is helping to set up support groups of people from a wide range of church background who want to take up the challenge of caring.

And so what projects are planned for the future?

The commitment to Romania will continue as strongly as before, and Albania remains a high priority. The situation in Yugoslavia is highly uncertain, but as long as aid is allowed into the country, and it can be taken without exposing volunteers to unnecessary danger, Blythswood will continue to operate there. An appeal has been made to the Society from Bulgaria, and this is an area which Jackie would very much like to help. In Poland, where there is not nearly the same degree of poverty, there is still great need, and the Society will continue to send clothes and other help; in particular, there is a need for warm clothing for elderly people as the harsh winter approaches. Blythswood will therefore keep its close connection with the Baptist Union in Poland.

Contact with pastors and other concerned people in Bulgaria has led Blythswood to a decision to send aid to Bulgaria before the end of 1992. These contacts will supply precise details of priority needs and suitable places where delivery can be made and storage and distribution facilities set up.

Blythswood has begun to work on some projects in association with Lady Nott, the wife of the Conservative Defence Secretary during the Falklands war. Herself a Slovenian, she has a deep concern for Yugoslavia and has raised substantial aid. Blythswood has taken van loads for her. Possibilities of joining forces with other, wealthier organisations to achieve specific objectives are being explored. The plight of the Iraqi marsh people is another need that the Society would like to help, and plans are being made with the Marshes Relief Organisation to raise money and aid and despatch it to them.

At Lochcarron, the work of Bible distribution and literature distribution continues, as parcels are sent out and students' questions marked. In a continent far away from the snows of Russia and the arid dust of Albania, Blythswood's ministry continues as it always has done; and in the streets of Britain and countries all over the world, you are quite likely to be offered a Blythswood tract or find one left in a library book.

The work is a whole. The line from the small group of friends who met - with some opposition at first from their Christian friends - because they had a deep concern for the spiritual needs of their nation, to the line of vehicles carrying bedding and food into war-torn Serbia and Croatia and the student reading *Let's Study Mark and Acts* in a college dormitory in Lagos, is a continuous one. Nothing has been abandoned; the vision is unchanged. Let us end as we began, with Jackie Ross and a vision for Christian literature.

> We take large quantities of Christian literature to Eastern Europe with us, and we try to make sure we always have some on board each vehicle. In Romania we have employed a translator, and we hope to employ an Albanian translator shortly. We hope to collaborate with Evangelical Press when they issue John Blanchard's *Ultimate Questions* in seven languages.
>
> I feel that material things ought not to be given as a sop to make Christian literature acceptable. That's repugnant! Often we give the literature to different people than those to whom we give the aid. But at the same time, I feel that aid shouldn't go in without, if at all possible, some Christian literature with it. The physical need is there, and that's what people are conscious of and want to help; but anything that will help them spiritually should be given too, because that is the need that will continue.

It is a need that the Blythswood has never been reluctant to spell out, not least to its own members. Jackie's article in the 1992 newsletter is typical: from a moving description of human tragedy in Yugoslavia, and an account of one of innumerable occasions when humanitarian aid had been given without the opportunity of, or insistence upon, evangelising those to whom the aid was given, he gives the reason in the following words.

> When we take aid to people in need they often ask, 'Why do you do it?' This gives us opportunity to tell them that many of those who work for us, and support by giving, do so out of love for Christ. They believe that Christ gave himself for them. They work and give out of love to Christ. In some circumstances it is possible to speak of what lasts. Jesus said, 'The bread of God is he which comes down from heaven, and gives life to the world ... I am the bread of life: he that comes to me shall never hunger; and he that believes on me shall never thirst.'
>
> If all your friends, possessions, religious teachers, church buildings and the externals of your religion were taken away from you, would you still really feel that you have everything you need in Christ Jesus? Would you still trust that the Bible speaks the truth when it says in Philippians 4:19, 'My God shall supply all your need according to his riches in glory by Christ Jesus'? Does thinking about Christ Jesus and all he has done for sinners give you more joy and happiness in your heart than anything else you can think of? If so, the Bible tells us heaven is a place for people like you. It is strange and frightening how so many people expect to go to heaven and have all sorts of pleasures and enjoyment there, totally unrelated to God and to what he tells us about himself in the Bible.
>
> Really trusting in the Lord Jesus Christ, learning to love him and following him in the way the Bible tells us to, brings joy and peace quite unlike anything else in this world. It is a taste of heaven. It brings us into a living relationship with him and we can say that we know the Lord. Then the thought of dying changes. It becomes the prospect of going home to be forever with someone whom we already know and love.

How about you? Would you feel at home in heaven? Do you look forward to meeting God? Does the idea of being perfectly holy appeal to you? Or would you feel a stranger in heaven and in God's company?

Are you willing to trust him? If not, what have you yourself got that is good enough to meet heaven's requirements? Remember that Jesus said, 'No man comes to the Father but by me.'

If good deeds were the royal highway to heaven, no fair-minded reader of this book could doubt that anybody working for Blythswood has done more than enough to qualify. The fact that good deeds are not enough is the reason for Blythswood's continued existence. It is the reason why Christian literature still sits side by side with food, medicine, clothes and agricultural supplies in Blythswood trucks. It is the reason that while the world suffers and people care enough to give and share and help and pray, the extraordinary story of Blythswood will go on.

If you would like to help the work of Blythswood, by donating money, goods or your time, please write or telephone: Blythswood, Lochcarron, Ross-shire Scotland IV54 8YD. Telephone : 05202 337

If you would like details of the Blythswood video, a sample set of Blythswood tracts, further information on Christianity, or a Bible free of charge, please write to the same address.

Blythswood is maintained entirely by donations.

# Appendix

## How to Plan a Relief Trip

Many who have read this book will have contemplated going themselves to Eastern Europe, taking relief and other help. This appendix is intended to provide some guidance based on the Blythswood's experiences over the years, though it does not claim to be definitive.

**Is your journey really necessary?**

This may seem a forbidding way to begin but it is an essential question and one you must ask yourself at the outset. One of the depressing experiences of taking relief to situations like those in Eastern Europe is to meet many very genuine people who have been moved by news reports and other awareness of the current needs and have decided to do something. Yet sadly they have often, unknowingly, invested time and money in duplicating effort needlessly, in purchasing goods and equipment that are not a priority in the country to which they are taken, or in solving problems and overcoming difficulties that have been solved long ago by others.

Ask yourself first, what is the precise purpose of your trip? Is it primarily aid, or is there an element of sightseeing or holidaying? The latter are not necessarily bad reasons to travel to Eastern Europe, but they need to be identified and separated from the humanitarian aspects. In fact there is a great need for Westerners to meet and befriend Eastern European on their own ground, for several of these countries have been isolated for decades and there is a good deal of mutual shyness to overcome.

If your prime motivation is delivering aid, however, you must ask several questions.

*1. Are you the only way of getting the goods delivered?*

It may be that an organisation already exists in your locality, or nationally, that would be willing to take goods collected by you to the destination of your choice. Some financial contribution may be requested, but it will be far less than the cost of taking it yourself.

It may be that no such organisation exists, or that those that do cannot go via your destination, or that other good reasons prevent your making use of an existing channel. If so, taking them yourself may be the right answer: but there are still questions to be asked.

*2. Are you taking the right goods?*

This is a crucial question. Many hours of effort setting up relief trips are wasted because the aid taken is unwanted or could have been made much more effective with only minor changes. Expensive toys, for example, can cause jealousy among children in institutions and are sometimes exhibited by the staff for the benefit of visitors rather than played with by the children. Simple stuffed balls and similar toys can often be much more useful.

But it's not so straightforward as that. Some institutions in Romania, for example, are now embarking on advanced programmes of physiotherapy and directed play with the children, supervised by trained staff who are working with limited facilities. In such cases a Lego set or other sophisticated toy will be welcomed and well used.

Medical supplies, too, can create frustration in hospitals where staff see stockpiles of short-life medicine building up with the distinct possibility of some of it being wasted, when severe shortages of some drugs easily obtainable in the West are causing major problems and threat to life. It should be remembered, however, that many groups and agencies have visited Eastern Europe and made wonderful promises of future aid which have never been honoured. As a result, hospitals are sometimes reluctant to use what they have received in the fear that no more will come; so the stockpiles are sometimes created by hospital policy rather than ill-judged giving. The only solution is to assure the recipients that future aid will come, and then to make sure it does. When some credibility has been gained, the hospital must be encouraged to make use of the medical supplies given, particularly if they have a finite shelf-life.

A further 'insurance policy' against failed promises from aid agencies is that often the same aid will be requested from a number of groups, in the hope that one at least will deliver. This is another good reason for building up a relationship of mutual trust as soon as possible, and perhaps also a reason for identifying with existing and proven aid agencies.

So how can one assess whether the goods are really wanted?

Firstly, any organisation working in the destination country will have a good idea of what is needed. Many organisations advertise in the Christian press and are good sources of information. Their UK headquarters will be able to provide details of their representatives in various countries. If you are not a Christian, don't assume that Christian organisations have nothing to offer you or vice-versa; in many of the Eastern European countries the churches are among the few agencies given humanitarian status by their government, or indeed which have any moral authority at all; where governments and government agencies have been discredited, and the people look back on years of lies and greed fed by leaders now disgraced, many of the churches that resisted such regimes are trusted, even if in some countries the trust is given only by the ethnic communities to which a particular church ministers.

Many who would like to give their time by taking aid to Eastern Europe are concerned by newspaper reports of aid being misused, or squandered because it is not wanted. Blythswood would be glad to suggest individuals, churches and institutions in Eastern Europe that are in genuine need and whose situation is well known to them. The address of Blythswood can be found on page 182.

**Preparation**

*1. Are you up-to-date?*

Situations change very rapidly and many individuals and organisations from many countries are involved in relief work. The newsletter you read three months ago may refer to situations that no longer exist; the family or church you visited last time or with whom you have been corresponding may have had its needs met by others. In the early days after the Romanian revolution, for example, the needs of a particular orphanage in Oradea were circulated quite widely in the West; most people obtained the information some time after the orphanage's needs had been met. Some time later, a relief truck visiting a home for the mentally disturbed near Sibiu found appalling poverty and primitive equipment; on a later visit, the home had been transformed by the work of a Dutch international relief organisation that had rebuilt many of its buildings and modernised the heating and other systems.

So if you have collected specific goods for a particular situation, make every effort to check whether the goods are still required. Be flexible, too, so that if you find when you arrive that the goods are no longer needed, be prepared to take them if requested elsewhere. In some countries storage is a major problem and surpluses can be time-consuming to distribute.

*2. Have you done your homework?*

It is unwise to travel to Eastern Europe without doing some basic reading about the situations you will meet. It is possible to put one's foot in it and cause oneself great embarrassment, but much more seriously it is possible, by a badly-informed remark, to inflame problems or even create them. The following points are worth bearing in mind.

*a. Avoid stereotyping*

One of the few certainties remaining after the 1989 revolutions in Eastern Europe is that there is, and never was, such a thing as 'Eastern Europe'. Communist domination imposed a regional identity, but the Eastern Bloc was only a political idea, never a geographical phenomenon. If you have visited one Eastern European country, don't be tempted to make assumptions about the others, whether it be regarding church life, family environment, agriculture or even embroidery!

An important aspect of this to remember is that within a country, different regions can be quite different. For example health authorities within the same country and answerable to the same government can have widely differing attitudes to medical help from the West, as at least one major international Christian relief project has discovered by experience.

If you are a Christian, be particularly cautious about making quick judgments about churches and congregations you visit. In the early days after the 1989 revolutions, many Western tourists visited Eastern European churches and rejoiced to find many churches singing the same choruses, reading the same authors and decorating their churches in the same way as their own churches did in the West. They identified these churches as 'evangelical' because they saw what they knew. Other churches, whose music sounds strange to Western ears, whose buildings are soberly decorated and whose preaching is sedate, were labelled by at least one British Christian newspaper as 'non-evangelical' - because the writer was unfamiliar with their externals. From the visitors' point of view this was unfortunate, because it made them miss some wonderful fellowship. From the Eastern church's point of view - much more seriously - it cut them off, having been pronounced 'unevangelical', from some important sources of aid.

There are many dead churches in Eastern Europe, just as there are in the West. It's not possible to spot which they are, however, by counting guitars or evaluating the murals!

*b. Read some history*

The media habitually compress and misrepresent the historical themes underlying the current events - conspicuously in the case of the Yugoslav war, where the long and bitter history of ethnic tension was not presented in the popular press until the conflict had been raging for many months. Read a brief modern history of the country you are going to, if only to identify areas of sensitivity that are best avoided in conversation. For many ethnic groups the twentieth-century post-war treaties are as contemporary as if the ink were still wet, and tempers flare easily. A particularly useful guide to the complexities of twentieth-century Europe is Hermann Kinder and Werner Hilgemann, *The Penguin Atlas of World History* vol. 2 (Penguin, 1978); this contains dozens of maps and useful notes. The religious background is well covered in Janice Broun's *Conscience and Captivity in Eastern Europe* (USA: Ethics & Public Policy Centre, 1988) and the quarterly journal *Religion in Communist Lands* (UK: Keston College).

It is not a theoretical issue. The ethnic history of most of the countries in the region is the primary cause of current unrest; the Yugoslav war, the tensions in Romania, the plight of minority communities in the Ukraine, the political disintegration of Czechoslovakia, all have their roots in ethnic bitterness and mistrust. You should be aware too that the churches are often intimately associated with ethnic groupings, and that reconciliation projects - of which there are several initiated by Christian agencies - have first to address the problems of resolving ethnic tensions.

**Travel arrangements**

To give detailed information here would be of limited use as situations change rapidly. Some organisations (such as the Romanian Aid Fund, 1 Catherine Court, Buckingham MK18 1UG) issue guidelines to help you plan the logistics of a trip.

For motoring advice, consult motoring organisations such as the AA, who can also advise on insurance and legal requirements when taking vehicles abroad. If you are taking a quantity of aid in anything bigger than a small van, it is well worth considering using a freight agent to prepare the paperwork for you. The fee to relief organisations is not large.

Take adequate spares and repair equipment for your vehicle, and check that it has efficient locks. Sign-painting the name of your organisation or project on the bodywork can speed you through some queues but red crosses should not be used, as this symbol is restricted to the official organisation and its agents.

Maps can be difficult to find, though the situation is becoming easier. In some countries it is virtually impossible to buy a map, so it is worth buying them before you leave if possible. Motoring atlases of Europe usually stop at Eastern Europe or change to an unusably small scale, but specialist map shops and larger high street book shops can often help. I bought excellent inexpensive maps of Hungary and Romania (Kummerly + Frey editions) from a large bookshop in England. Language can be a problem; you are not likely to find Romanian maps that give the place names in Hungarian or German (such maps were illegal in Ceausescu's time), and it can be disconcerting to find Albania called 'Shqiperia' on local maps.

A number of travel guides and travel books about Eastern Europe are beginning to appear. Many of them are unrealistically optimistic and read like travel agent's brochures; even the best are quickly out of date. Better than most is Simon Calder's *Travellers' Survival Kit: Soviet Union and Eastern Europe* (UK: Vacation Work, 1989).

When choosing travel companions and helpers, be aware that travel to these countries can be an emotional and disorientating experience. Make sure that one person is acknowledged leader of the trip, and think hard before taking anybody with a problem of anger, intolerance, or emotional insecurity. A sense of humour is an asset.

### Practical matters

Most of the practical aspects of ensuring as trouble-free a trip as possible are matters of common sense and sensitivity. The following are some selected tips from Blythswood experience and that of the author.

*1. Money*

Don't take large-denomination Travellers Cheques. In countries such as Romania, Albania and what was Yugoslavia there is very little to spend money on and there are often regulations against taking surplus currency in and out. Twenty-five pound cheques should be ample for a group. If you have reasonably secure storage, it is usually better to take bank notes - dollars are usually very acceptable, and German Deutschemarks and British sterling are usually acceptable depending on the state of the financial markets at the time.

You will certainly be approached by black-market currency changers. Apart from the moral aspects, the chance of being swindled with counterfeit notes and the fact that it could well get you into trouble with the police, dealing with black marketeers is unwise as in Romania, for example, payment for hotel accommodation in lei must be accompanied by your official currency receipt, and in Hungary possession of a currency receipt enables you to change money back on leaving the country. If you wish to give gifts of money, give Western currency (many people are embarrassed by such gifts, so be sensitive). As you are unlikely to get a good exchange rate, any local currency you obtain will probably not be as much use to your friends.

*2. Gifts*

A small gift to one's hosts is always appreciated. People who have visited the country before can usually give good advice. A pastor who has just taken delivery of a thousand pound's worth of Bibles will probably be delighted to receive a package of chocolate digestive biscuits and some good coffee. A personal gift which has obviously cost the giver a great deal of money in the West is likely to cause embarrassment - better to meet such needs as part of the relief goods supplied. Pictorial tea-towels, calendars, photographs of your children and similar gifts are much appreciated. It is usually possible to find out in advance if anything is particularly difficult to obtain in the country you are visiting - in Romania, for example, sellotape, biros, nail scissors and jigsaws are all equally scarce. If I am flying to Eastern Europe I usually try to pick up several bars of flower- and fruit-scented soap at the airport when I leave England, as cosmetics and soaps are often very difficult to find in Eastern Europe and such gifts are very welcome. For Christians who can read English, recent theological and biblical paperbacks are always appreciated, and will be passed around the whole church.

*3. Hospitality*

In most countries, to refuse any food placed in front of you causes great offence, though your hosts will probably not show it. Food is one of the few gifts they can give, often by queuing for hours to buy it. If you have brought gifts of food, give them while leaving, or you will be expected to sit down and eat most of your own gift there and then. Often a family will sit watching their guests eat; this is embarrassing, especially when what you are eating would provide three or four meals. There is really no option to but to eat and be thankful.

Conversely, be sensitive when entertaining others or when using hotels or restaurants. Many Eastern European Christians have been horrified to see Westerners eating their way through the equivalent of an entire month's pastor's salary in a single meal, or living in what to them is incredible luxury. As hard currency buys a lot in Eastern Europe, it is easy to spend what seems very little and yet cause offence.

Some Eastern European food is difficult for Westerners to manage, either because it is exotic or because it is of poor quality and possibly unhygienic. Take plenty of medicine with you for stomach upsets. In Romania, never eat ice-cream (unless it is served by your hosts, in which case you will have to take the risk of an unpleasant few hours to follow).

*4. Smoking and alcohol*

Eastern Europe has not had the same anti-tobacco education that the West has had, and the very real dangers are not well publicised; for many it is one of the few affordable luxuries. Many Christians smoke heavily (some denominations more than others). Well-meaning exhortations to give up smoking can cause great offence. Most smokers are far more courteous than Western smokers, incidentally, and will readily extinguish a cigarette if it is bothering others.

Alcohol is not acceptable in some denominations, and is freely taken in others. The wine and spirits are often potent, though it is rare to see a social drinker intoxicated, though alcoholism is a major problem in most countries. Even if you are not a teetotaller it would be wise to resist invitations to drain your glass at a single gulp - the correct way to drink in many circles. Sometimes you will be given a freshly opened bottle of wine and be expected to drink it all yourself at a single sitting. Your hosts may well be offended if you refuse, but it is better to offend on this issue than find yourself drunk. Moderate drinkers would do well to avoid East

European spirits altogether. Teetotalism, even if only for the purposes of the trip, has much to commend it. It should go without saying that driving and drinking is quite unacceptable.

Similar sensitivity, incidentally, should govern choice of clothes, especially in seaside resorts and on sunny days; what is acceptable in Britain may not be acceptable abroad.

*5. Good listening*

Be sensitive to your hosts who may have had several Western visitors that month already. Many pastors who speak English are drained by constant demands on their hospitality, and not just in the financial sense.

If your host prepares breakfast in bed for you it is probably because the family wants to be on their own. Don't protest; it may be one of the few opportunities they have. Do not expect to automatically be invited to preach in church: some pastors rarely preach in their own churches in the summer because they feel obliged to offer the pulpit to visitors each week.

Spend time listening. Many of the people you will meet are heroes of the faith and have endured experiences we cannot imagine.

*5. Languages*

German is quite widely spoken in some areas; French is useful in Romania. If available for the language you require, the Berlitz *For Travellers* pocketbooks are helpful. Some come with audio tapes - a painless way of learning enough Hungarian to impress your hosts. You will find that most people will be delighted to try out their English on you.

*6. Queuing*

It is accepted in many situations that Westerners and non-nationals will go to the head of any queue. This applies, for example, at customs posts. It will also be tolerated in many banks and train stations, though most Britishers will find it acutely embarrassing when their host drags them past old men and women who have probably been waiting hours.

*7. First Aid and Medicine*

Vaccinations are not compulsory for Eastern Europe. Your doctor at home may advise a particular vaccine as a precaution. In any case, take a full first-aid kit, including sterile dressings, hypodermic needles and (if possible) blood plasma, and leave it behind for your hosts when you leave. Painkillers of all kinds and antibiotics are difficult to find and are very much appreciated as presents, as are vitamin tablets in child dosages. If you do need an injection or blood transfusion, insist that the doctor uses the needles you brought. Re-use, with possible infection, is common in some countries, and the AIDS problem is immense.

*8. If Things Go Wrong*

Before you leave home, find out the address of the British Embassy and its telephone number for each of the countries you are going to.

Find out what the dialling code is to ring home from telephones in the countries you are visiting, and also how to use their telephone system. In Hungary, for instance, you need one code to dial another town and a different code to dial internationally; there are rarely any English-language code books, instruction or operators available.

Check the procedures to be followed if your vehicle breaks down or if you have an accident (bear in mind that some insurance will not extend beyond EEC boundaries). Ask your bank about procedures for drawing emergency cash from your account when in Eastern Europe. Hotels can often help in emergency bureau de change facilities (and the transaction will be legal). If you run into major financial problems, go to a local branch of any Western bank; if they are unable to help go to your embassy. In some countries, you can send a fax from a bank, and (in Hungary, for example) there are quite efficient fax and telex bureaux open until fairly late in the evening.

The British Government (Department of Trade and Industry, British Overseas Trade Board) publish a series of *Hints for Exporters Visiting ...* which contain useful information about services and government agencies in a wide range of countries, as well as much helpful detail on local practices, holidays, customs, etiquette etc.

Tell your relatives not to worry if they receive no telephone calls or postcards while you are in Eastern Europe. Telephoning is often impossible, and you are quite likely to arrive home before the postcard does.